80 Campfire Songs

for Tin Whistle

Thomas Balinger
80 Campfire Songs for Tin Whistle
Cover photograph: © bernardbodo - Fotolia.com

© 2018

ISBN: 9781730987847

Preface

Hello fellow Tin Whistle players,

welcome to this songbook for Tin Whistle in D.
On the following pages I've collected songs known and loved the world over.
These songs cover a wide musical range so I'm sure you'll find lots of songs you'll enjoy playing.
All songs have been arranged for the beginning to intermediate player.
To further facilitate playing I added tin whistle tablature to the standard notation.
This handy form of graphical notation shows you exactly how to play every note–reading music not required. I added chord symbols to all songs so you can play them together with others. You'll find the chord diagrams for guitar right next to each song.
I also included a fingering chart for tin whistle as well as the basic guitar chords and a selection of easy picking and strumming patterns for song accompaniment.

Wishing you lots of fun with these songs,
Thomas Balinger

PS. Players interested in ornamentation (embellishing the melody of a song) will find a short introduction to this playing technique in the appendix.

Contents

Appendix

Cotton-eyed Joe

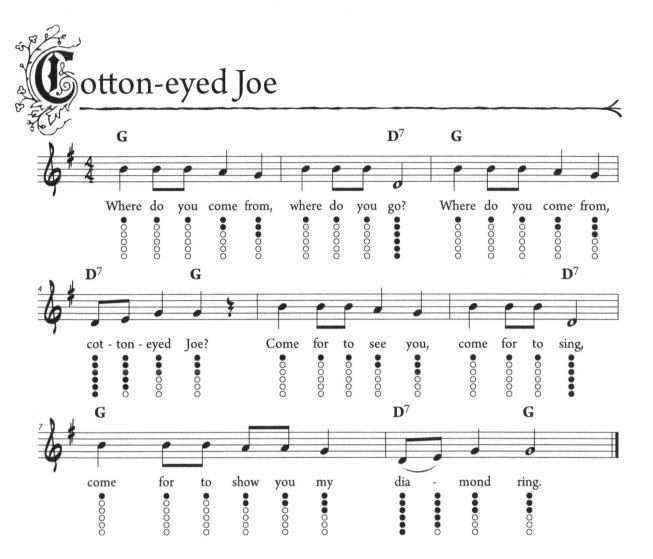

Where do you come from, where do you go? Where do you come from, cot-ton-eyed Joe? Come for to see you, come for to sing, come for to show you my dia - mond ring.

2. *Do you remember a long time ago,*
   there was a man called cotton-eyed Joe?
   Could have been married a long time ago,
   hadn't it been for cotton-eyed Joe.

3. *Old bull fiddle and a shoe-string bow,*
   wouldn't play nothin' like cotton-eyed Joe.
   Play it fast or play it slow,
   can't play nothin' like cotton-eyed Joe.

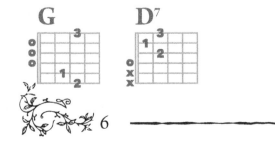

Red river valley

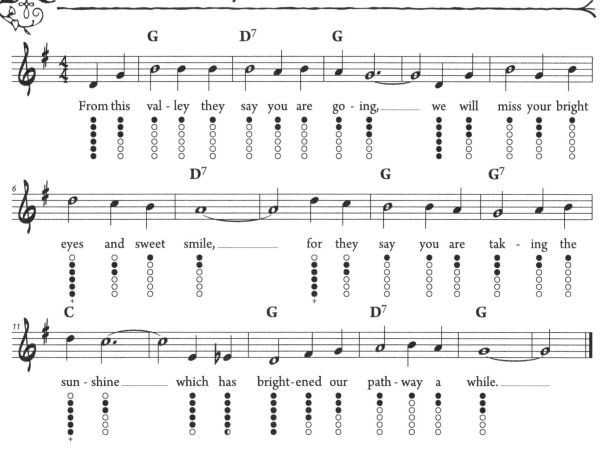

From this val - ley they say you are go - ing, _____ we will miss your bright eyes and sweet smile, _____ for they say you are tak - ing the sun - shine _____ which has bright-ened our path - way a while. _____

2. Come and sit by my side if you love me;
   Do not hasten to bid me adieu,
   but remember the Red River Valley,
   and the girl that has loved you so true.

3. I've been thinking a long time, my darling,
   of the sweet words you never would say,
   now, alas, must my fond hopes all vanish?
   For they say you are going away.

4. Won't you think of the valley you're leaving,
   oh, how lonely and sad it will be,
   just think of the fond heart you're breaking,
   and the grief you are causing to me.

5. From this valley they say you are going,
   when you go, may your darling go too?
   Would you leave her behind unprotected,
   when she loves no one other than you.

6. As you go to your home by the ocean,
   may you never forget those sweet hours,
   that we spent in the Red River Valley,
   and the love we exchanged ,mid the flowers.

7. I have promised you, darling, that never
   will a word from my lips cause you pain,
   and my life, it will be yours forever,
   if you only will love me again.

8. They will bury me where you have wandered,
   near the hills where the daffodils grow,
   when you're gone from the Red River valley,
   for I can't live without you I know.

G   **D⁷**   **C**

Tom Dooley

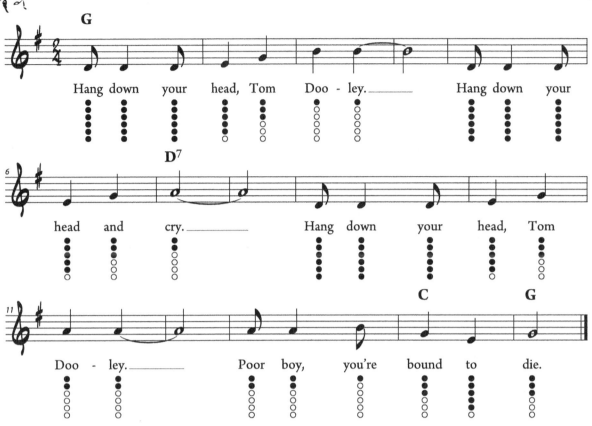

Hang down your head, Tom Doo - ley.____ Hang down your

head and cry.____ Hang down your head, Tom

Doo - ley.____ Poor boy, you're bound to die.

2. *This time tomorrow,*
   reckon where I'll be?
   If it hadn't been for Grayson,
   I'd a-been in Tennessee.

3. *This time tomorrow,*
   reckon where I'll be?
   Down in some lonesome valley,
   hangin' from a white oak tree.

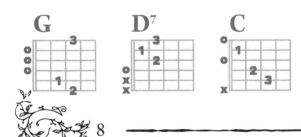

Away in a manger

A - way in a man - ger, no crib for His bed, the litt - le Lord
Je - sus laid down His sweet head. The stars in the bright sky looked down where He
lay, the lit - tle Lord Je - sus, a - sleep on the hay.

2. The cattle are lowing
   the poor Baby wakes.
   But little Lord Jesus
   no crying He makes.
   I love Thee, Lord Jesus,
   look down from the sky
   and stay by my side,
   'til morning is nigh.

3. Be near me, Lord Jesus,
   I ask Thee to stay.
   Close by me forever
   and love me I pray.
   Bless all the dear children
   in Thy tender care
   and take us to heaven
   to live with Thee there.

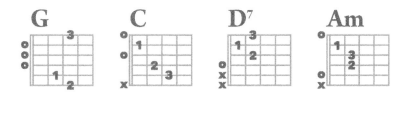

Banks of the Ohio

2. I held a knife against her breast
   as into my arms she pressed,
   "Willie, oh Willie, don't murder me,
   I'm not prepared for eternity."

3. I started home 'twist twelve and one,
   crying "My God! What have I done?
   Killed the only woman I loved,
   because she would not be my bride."

The John B. sails

1. Come on the sloop John B.,
   my grandfather and me,
   round Nassau town we did roam.
   Drinking all night, we got in a fight,
   we feel so break-up, we want to go home.

Chorus
   So hoist up the John B. sails,
   see how the mainsail set,
   send for the captain ashore, let me go home,
   let me go home, let me go home,
   I feel so break-up, I want to go home.

2. The first mate he got drunk,
   break up the people trunk,
   constable come aboard, take him away,
   Mr. Johnstone, leave me alone,
   I feel so break-up, I want to go home.

3. The poor cook got the fits,
   throw away all o' my grits,
   captain's pig done eat up all o' my corn.
   Lemme go home, I want to go home,
   I feel so break-up, I want to go home.

4. Steamboat go by steam,
   sailboat go by sail,
   my girl's hat ain't got no tail.
   Lemme go home, I want to go home,
   I feel so break-up, I want to go home.

5. Send all the things from ashore,
   let all the breezes blow,
   I'm so sorry that I can longer stay,
   good-by to you, Tra-la-la-lu,
   this is the worst trip since I was born.

G   **D**   **C**

Sweet Betsy from Pike

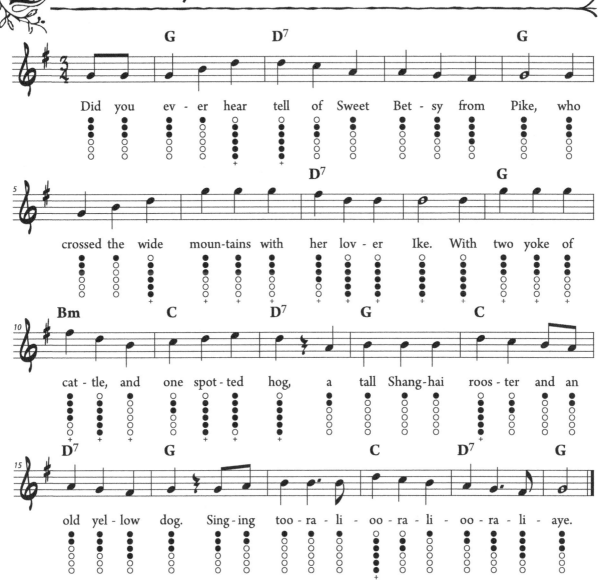

2. They swam the wide rivers and crossed the tall peaks,
and camped on the prairie for weeks upon weeks.
Starvation and cholera, hard work and slaughter –
they reached California, spite of hell and high water.
Singing too-ra-li-oo-ra-li-oo-ra-li-ay.

3. One evening quite early they camped on the Platte,
twas near by the road on a green shady flat.
Betsy, sore-footed, lay down to repose –
with wonder Ike gazed on that Pike County rose.
Singing too-ra-li-oo-ra-li-oo-ra-li-ay.

4. The Injuns came down in a thundering horde,
and Betsy was scared they would scalp her adored.
So under the wagon-bed Betsy did crawl
and she fought off the Injuns with musket and ball.
Singing too-ra-li-oo-ra-li-oo-ra-li-ay.

5. The wagon broke down with a terrible crash,
and out on the prairie rolled all sorts of trash.
A few little baby-clothes, done up with care,
looked rather suspicious, but all on the square.
Singing too-ra-li-oo-ra-li-oo-ra-li-ay.

6. They stopped at Salt Lake to inquire of the way,
   when Brigham declared that Sweet Betsy should stay.
   Betsy got frightened and ran like a deer,
   while Brigham stood pawing the ground like a steer.
   Singing too-ra-li-oo-ra-li-oo-ra-li-ay.

7. The alkali desert was burning and bare,
   and Isaac's soul shrank from the death that lurked there.
   "Dear old Pike County, I'll go back to you" –
   says Betsy, "You'll go by yourself if you do!"
   Singing too-ra-li-oo-ra-li-oo-ra-li-ay.

8. They soon reached the desert, where Betsy gave out,
   and down in the sand she lay rolling about.
   Ike in great wonder looked on in surprise,
   saying, "Betsy, get up, you'll get sand in your eyes."
   Singing too-ra-li-oo-ra-li-oo-ra-li-ay.

9. Sweet Betsy got up in a great deal of pain.
   She declared she'd go back to Pike County again.
   Ike gave a sigh, and they fondly embraced,
   and they traveled along with his arm round her waist.
   Singing too-ra-li-oo-ra-li-oo-ra-li-ay.

10. The Shanghai ran off, and the cattle all died,
    that morning the last piece of bacon was fried.
    Ike got discouraged, Betsy got mad,
    the dog drooped his tail and looked wonderfully sad.
    Singing too-ra-li-oo-ra-li-oo-ra-li-ay.

11. They suddenly stopped on a very high hill,
    with wonder looked down upon old Placerville.
    Ike said to Betsy, as he cast his eyes down,
    "Sweet Betsy, my darling, we've got to Hangtown."
    Singing too-ra-li-oo-ra-li-oo-ra-li-ay.

12. Long Ike and Sweet Betsy attended a dance.
    Ike wore a pair of his Pike County pants.
    Betsy was covered with ribbons and rings.
    Says Ike, "You're an angel, but where is your wings?"
    Singing too-ra-li-oo-ra-li-oo-ra-li-ay.

13. A miner said, "Betsy, will you dance with me?"
    "I will that, old hoss, if you don't make too free.
    Don't dance me hard, do you want to know why?
    Doggone you, I'm chock-full of strong alkali."
    Singing too-ra-li-oo-ra-li-oo-ra-li-ay.

14. This Pike County couple got married, of course,
    but Ike became jealous, and obtained a divorce.
    Betsy, well-satisfied, said with a shout,
    "Goodby, you big lummox, I'm glad you backed out!"
    Singing too-ra-li-oo-ra-li-oo-ra-li-ay.

G   **D⁷**   **Bm** 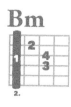 **C**

Brahms' lullaby

Lull - a - by, and good night, with ___ pink ros - es be - dight, with ___ lil - ies o - ver spread, is my ba - by's sweet head. Lay thee down now and rest, may thy slum - ber be blessed! Lay thee down now and rest, may thy slum - ber be blessed!

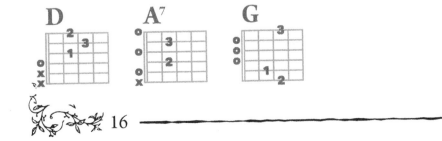

 Whiskey Johnny

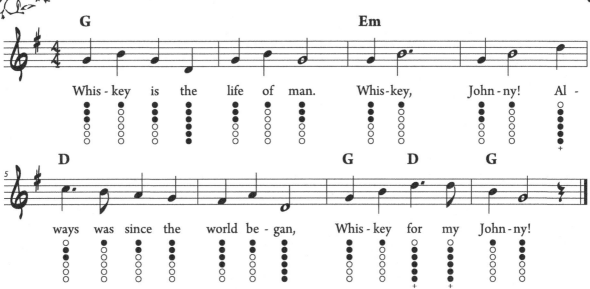

Whis-key is the life of man. Whis-key, John-ny! Al-ways was since the world be-gan, Whis-key for my John-ny!

2. Whiskey here, whiskey there,
   whiskey almost everywhere.

3. Whiskey up and whiskey down,
   whiskey all around the town.

4. Whiskey killed me poor old dad,
   whiskey drove me mother mad.

5. My wife and I do not agree,
   she puts whiskey in her tea.

6. I had a girl and her name was Lize,
   she puts whiskey in her pies.

7. Oh whiskey straight, and whiskey strong,
   give me some whiskey and I'll sing you a song.

8. If whiskey comes too near my nose,
   I tip it up and down she goes.

9. Some likes whiskey, some likes beer,
   I wish I had a barrel here.

10. Whiskey made me pawn me clothes,
    whiskey gave me this broken nose

11. Oh the mate likes whiskey, the skipper likes rum,
    the sailors like both but me can't get none

12. Whiskey is the life of man,
    whiskey from that old tin can.

13. I thought I heard the first mate say,
    I treats me crew in a decent way.

14. If whiskey was a river and I could swim,
    I'd say here goes and dive right in.

15. If whiskey was a river and I was a duck
    I'd dive to the bottom and never come up

16. I wisht I knew where whiskey grew,
    I'd eat the leaves and the branches too.

17. A tot of whiskey all around
    and a bottle full for the shanty man.

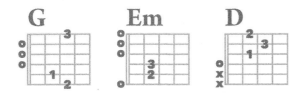

Waltzing Matilda

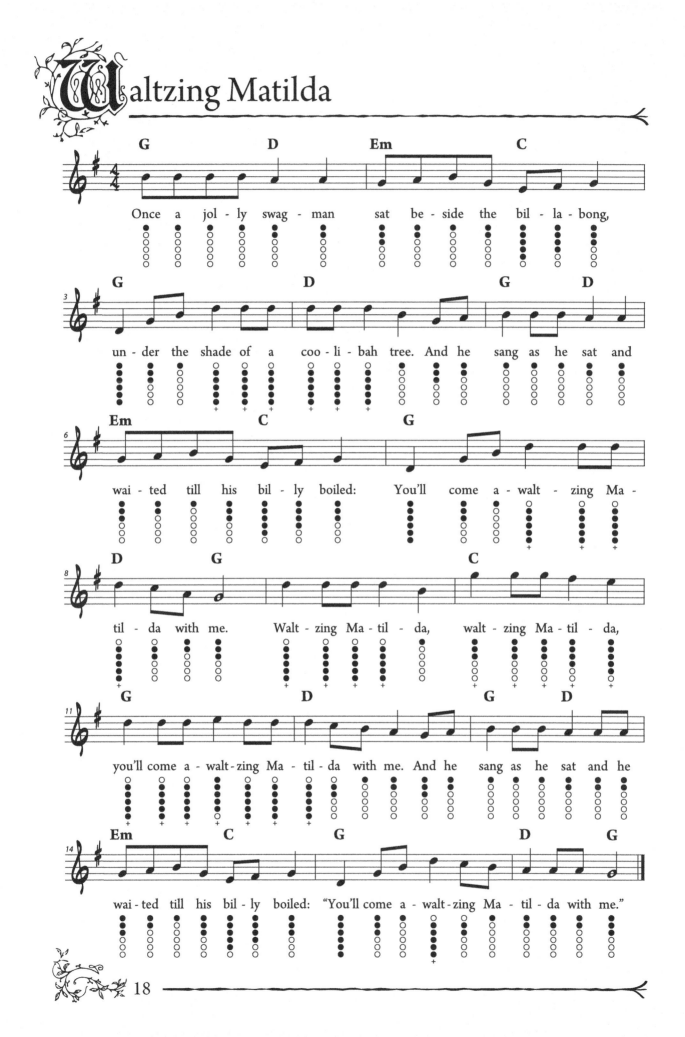

2. Down came a jumbuck to drink at that billabong.
   Up jumped the swagman and grabbed him with glee.
   And he sang as he shoved that jumbuck in his tucker bag:
   "You'll come a-waltzing Matilda, with me."
   Waltzing Matilda, waltzing Matilda
   "You'll come a-waltzing Matilda, with me",
   And he sang as he shoved that jumbuck in his tucker bag:
   "You'll come a-waltzing Matilda, with me."

3. Up rode the squatter, mounted on his thoroughbred.
   Down came the troopers, one, two, and three.
   "Whose is that jumbuck you've got in your tucker bag?
   You'll come a-waltzing Matilda, with me."
   Waltzing Matilda, waltzing Matilda
   "You'll come a-waltzing Matilda, with me",
   "Whose is that jumbuck you've got in your tucker bag?
   You'll come a-waltzing Matilda, with me."

4. Up jumped the swagman and sprang into the billabong.
   "You'll never take me alive!" said he
   And his ghost may be heard as you pass by that billabong:
   "Who'll come a-waltzing Matilda, with me?"
   Waltzing Matilda, waltzing Matilda
   "You'll come a-waltzing Matilda, with me",
   And his ghost may be heard as you pass by that billabong:
   "Who'll come a-waltzing Matilda, with me?"

G   **D**   **Em**   **C**

Yankee Doodle

2. Father and I went down to camp,
   along with Captain Gooding.
   And there we saw the men and boys,
   as thick as hasty pudding.
   Yankee Doodle, keep it up,
   Yankee Doodle dandy.
   Mind the music and the step,
   and with the girls be handy.

3. There was Captain Washington,
   upon a slapping stallion.
   A-giving orders to his men,
   I guess there was a million.
   Yankee Doodle, keep it up,
   Yankee Doodle dandy.
   Mind the music and the step,
   and with the girls be handy.

4. Yankee Doodle is a tune,
   that comes in mighty handy,
   The enemies all run away,
   at Yankee Doodle dandy!
   Yankee Doodle, keep it up,
   Yankee Doodle dandy.
   Mind the music and the step,
   and with the girls be handy.

D **A** **D⁷** **G** 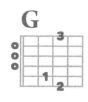 **A⁷**

2. *I have seen Him in the watch-fires of a hundred circling camps,*
   they have builded Him an altar in the evening dews and damps;
   I can read His righteous sentence by the dim and flaring lamps:
   His day is marching on.
   Glory, glory, hallelujah! ...

3. *I have read a fiery gospel writ in burnished rows of steel:*
   "As ye deal with my contemners, so with you my grace shall deal;
   Let the Hero, born of woman, crush the serpent with His heel,
   since God is marching on."
   Glory, glory, hallelujah! ...

4. *He has sounded forth the trumpet that shall never call retreat;*
   He is sifting out the hearts of men before His judgment-seat:
   Oh, be swift, my soul, to answer Him! Be jubilant, my feet!
   Our God is marching on.
   Glory, glory, hallelujah! ...

5. *In the beauty of the lilies Christ was born across the sea,*
   with a glory in His bosom that transfigures you and me:
   As he died to make men holy, let us die to make men free,
   while God is marching on.
   Glory, glory, hallelujah! ...

6. *He is coming like the glory of the morning on the wave,*
   he is wisdom to the mighty, He is honour to the brave;
   So the world shall be His footstool, and the soul of wrong His slave,
   our God is marching on.
   Glory, glory, hallelujah! ...

C   **F**   **E**   **Am**   **G⁷**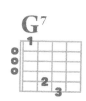

Aura Lee

As the black-bird in the spring, 'neath the wil-low tree,

sat and piped, I heard him sing, prais-ing Au-ra Lee.

Au - ra Lee! Au - ra Lee! Maid of gold - en hair,

sun - shine came a - long with thee and swall-ows in the air.

2. In thy blush the rose was born,
   music, when you spake,
   through thine azure eye the morn,
   sparkling seemed to break.
   Aura Lee, Aura Lee,
   birds of crimson wing,
   never song have sung to me,
   as in that sweet spring.
   Aura Lee! Aura Lee! ...

3. Aura Lee, the bird may flee,
   the willow's golden hair,
   swing through winter fitfully,
   on the stormy air.
   Yet if thy blue eyes I see,
   gloom will soon depart;
   for to me, sweet Aura Lee
   is sunshine through the heart.
   Aura Lee! Aura Lee! ...

4. When the mistletoe was green,
   midst the winter's snows,
   sunshine in thy face was seen,
   kissing lips of rose.
   Aura Lee, Aura Lee,
   Take my golden ring;
   Love and light return with thee,
   and swallows with the spring.
   Aura Lee! Aura Lee! ...

G   **Am**   **D⁷**   **B⁷**   **Em**   **G⁷**

C   **Cm** 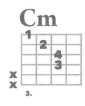 **A⁷**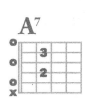

The first noel

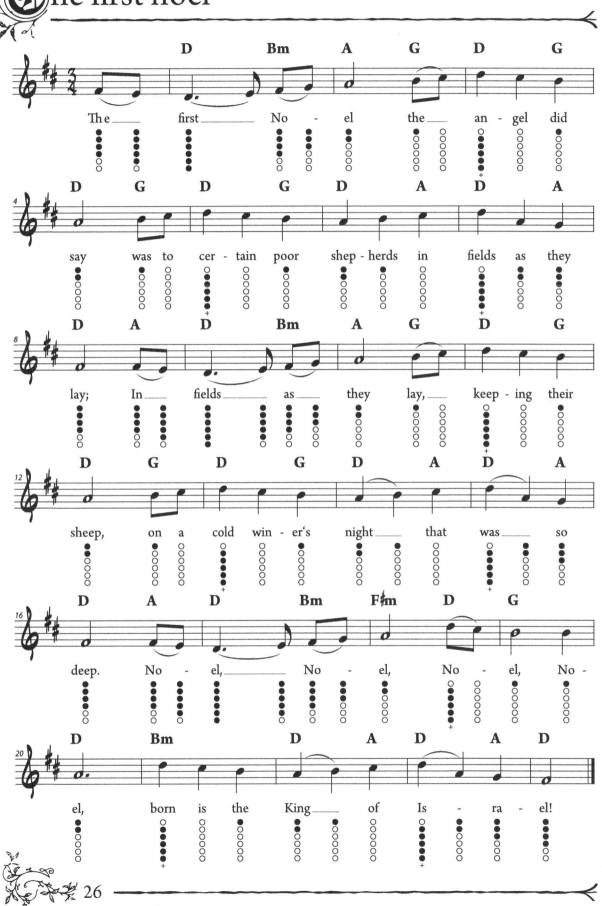

2. They looked up and saw a star
   shining in the east beyond them far,
   and to the earth it gave great light,
   and so it continued both day and night.

3. And by the light of that same star,
   three wise men came from country far;
   To seek for a king was their intent,
   and to follow the star wherever it went.

4. This star drew nigh to the northwest,
   o'er Bethlehem it took it rest,
   and there it did both stop and stay
   right over the place where Jesus lay.

5. Then entered in those wise men three
   full reverently upon their knee,
   and offered there in his presence
   their gold, and myrrh, and frankincense.

6. Then let us all with one accord
   sing praises to our heavenly Lord;
   That hath made heaven and earth of naught,
   and with his blood mankind hath bought.

 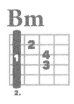  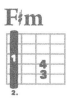

Auld lang syne

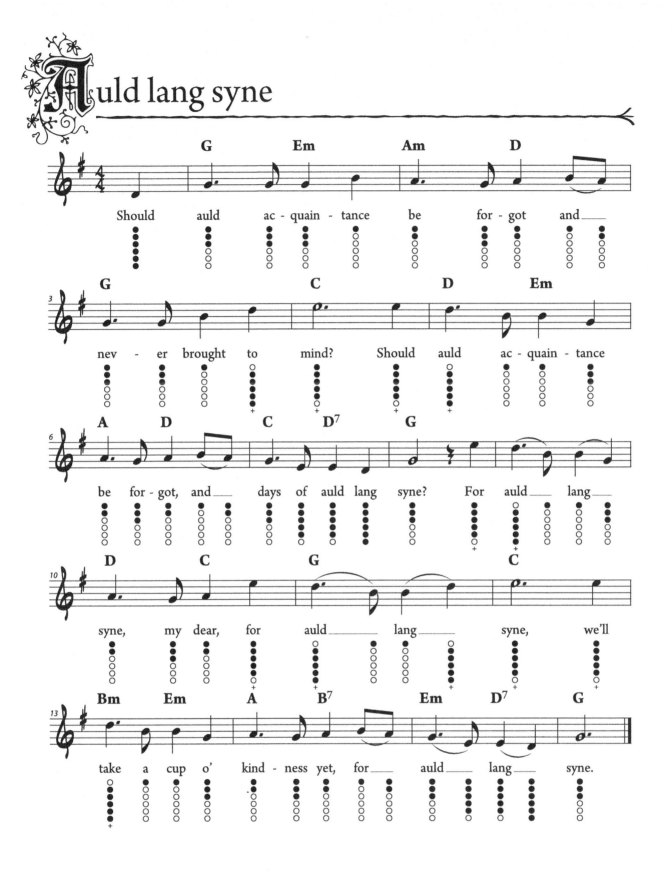

Chorus:
For auld lang syne, my dear,
for auld lang syne,
we'll take a cup o' kindness yet,
for auld lang syne.

2. *And surely ye'll be your pint-stoup!*
   and surely I'll be mine!
   And we'll tak' a cup o' kindness yet,
   for auld lang syne.

3. *We twa hae run about the braes,*
   and pou'd the gowans fine;
   But we've wander'd mony a weary fit,
   sin' auld lang syne.

4. *We twa hae paidl'd in the burn,*
   frae morning sun till dine;
   But seas between us braid hae roar'd
   sin' auld lang syne.

5. *And there's a hand, my trusty fiere!*
   and gie's a hand o' thine!
   And we'll tak' a right gude-willie waught,
   for auld lang syne.

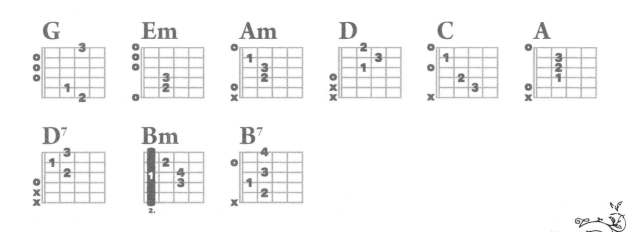

We wish you a merry Christmas

2. *Now bring us some figgy pudding,*
   now bring us some figgy pudding,
   now bring us some figgy pudding,
   and bring some out here!

3. *For we all like figgy pudding,*
   we all like figgy pudding,
   we all like figgy pudding,
   so bring some out here!

4. *And we won't go until we've got some,*
   we won't go until we've got some,
   we won't go until we've got some,
   so bring some out here!

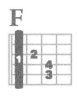

Banks of Allan Water

2. On the banks of Allan Water,
   when brown autumn spread his store.
   There I saw the miller's daughter,
   but she smiled no more.
   For the summer, grief had brought her
   and the soldier false was he,
   on the banks of Allan Water,
   none so sad as she.

3. On the banks of Allan Water,
   when the winter snow fell fast.
   Still was seen the miller's daughter
   chilling blew the blast.
   But the miller's lovely daughter,
   both from cold and care was free.
   On the banks of Allan Water
   there a corpse lay she.

C   G   F

silent night

2. Silent night, Holy night!
Son of God, love's pure light.
Radiant beams from thy holy face.
With the dawn of redeeming grace,
Jesus, Lord at thy birth,
Jesus, Lord at thy birth.

3. Silent night, Holy night!
Shepherds quake at the sight.
Glories stream from heaven above.
Heavenly hosts sing Hallelujah,
Christ the Savior is born,
Christ the Savior is born.

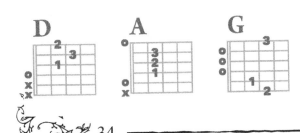

Roll in my sweet baby's arms

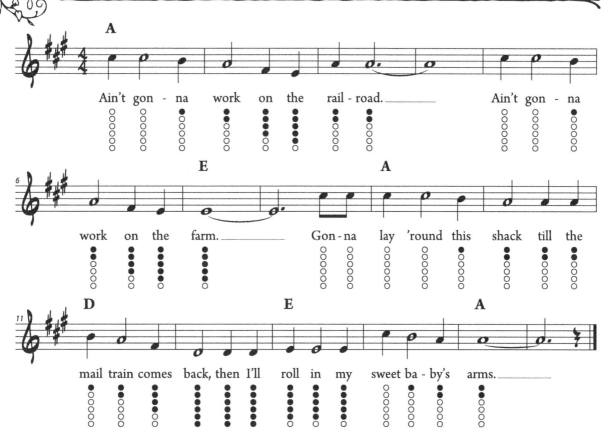

2. *Now where was you last Friday night while I was lyin' in jail.*
   Walkin' the streets with another man you wouldn't even go my bail,
   then I'll roll in my sweet baby's arms.

3. *I know your parent don't like me they drove me away from your door.*
   And my life's too bluer never to wearing more,
   then I'll roll in my sweet baby's arms.

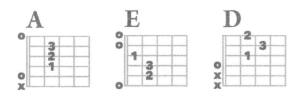

The streets of Laredo

2. Oh beat the drums slowly and play the fife lowly;
   Sing the Death March as you carry me along.
   Take me to the valley, there lay the sod o'er me,
   I'm a young cowboy and know I've done wrong.

3. I see by your outfit that you are a cowboy.
   These words he did say as I boldly walked by.
   Come sit down beside me and hear my sad story;
   Got shot in the breast and I know I must die!

4. My friends and relations they live in the Nation:
   They know not where their dear boy has gone.
   I first came to Texas and hired to a ranchman,
   I'm a young cowboy and I know I've done wrong.

5. It was once in the saddle I used to go dashing:
   It was once in the saddle I used to go gay.
   First to the dram house and then to the card house,
   got shot in the breast and I'm dying today.

6. Get six jolly cowboys to carry my coffin;
   Get six pretty maidens to sing me a song.
   Put bunches of roses all over my coffin,
   put roses to deaden the cods as they fall.

7. Go gather around you a group of young cowboys,
   and tell them the story of this my sad fate.
   Tell one and the other before they go further,
   to stop their wild roving before it's too late.

8. Go fetch me some water, a cool cup of water
   to cool my parched lips, then the poor cowboy said.
   Before I returned his spirit had left him
   Had gone to his Maker, the cowboy was dead.

9. We beat the drum slowly and played the fife lowly,
   and bitterly wept as we bore him along.
   For awe all loved our comrade, so brave, young, and handsome,
   we all loved our comrade although he'd done wrong.

G **C** **D** **Em** **Am** **D⁷**

Clementine

2. Light she was, and like a fairy,
   and her shoes were number nine,
   herring boxes without topses,
   sandals were for Clementine.

3. Drove she ducklings to the water
   every morning just at nine,
   struck her foot agains a splinter,
   fell into the foaming brine.

4. Rosy lips above the water,
   blowing bubbles mighty fine,
   but, alas, I was no swimmer,
   so I lost my Clementine.

5. How I missed her! How I missed her!
   How I missed my Clementine!
   But I kissed her little sister,
   and forgot my Clementine.

G **E⁷** **Am** **D⁷**

Amazing Grace

1. A - maz - ing Grace how sweet the sounds, that saved a wretch like me. I once was lost, but now am found; was blind but now I see.

2. 'Twas grace that taught my heart to fear,
   and grace my fear relived.
   How precious did that grace appear,
   the hour I first believed.

3. When we've been there ten thousand years,
   bright shining as the sun.
   We've no less days to sing God's praise,
   than when we first begun.

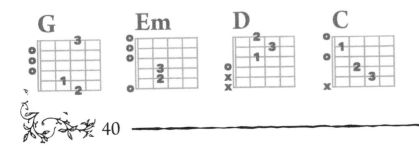

Bury me beneath the willow

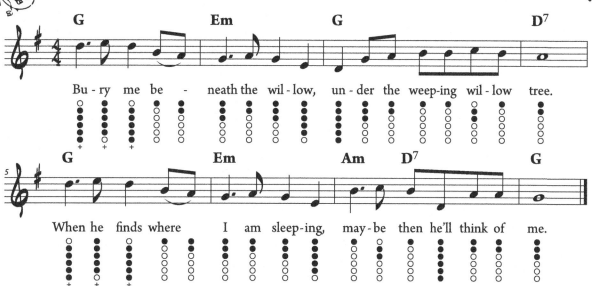

Bu - ry me be - neath the wil - low, un - der the weep-ing wil - low tree.

When he finds where I am sleep-ing, may - be then he'll think of me.

2. My heart is sad I am lonely,
   for the only one I love.
   When shall I see her oh no never,
   'til we meet in heaven above.

3. She told me that she dearly loved me.
   How could I believe it untrue,
   until the angels softly whispered,
   she will prove untrue to you.

4. Tomorrow was to be our wedding,
   God, oh God, where can she be.
   She's out a courting with another,
   and no longer cares for me

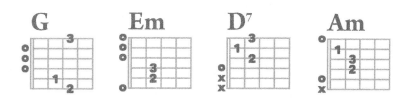

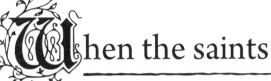

When the saints

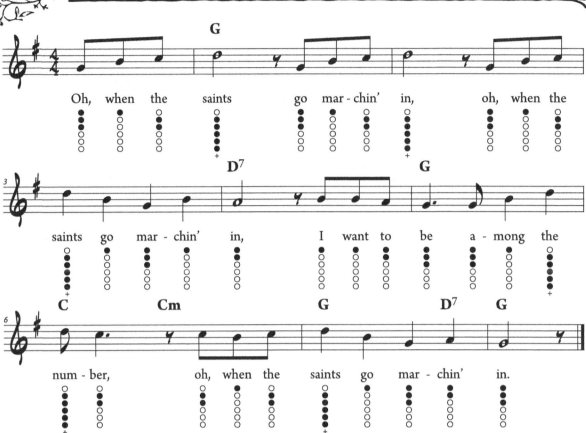

2. And when the stars begin to shine ...

3. And when the band begins to play ...

4. When Gabriel blows in his horn ...

5. And when the sun refuses to shine ...

6. And when they crown Him Lord of Lords ...

7. And on that halleluja-day ...

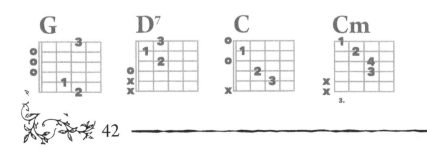

On top of Old Smokey

On top of old Smo - key, all cov - ered with snow; I lost my true lov - er a - court - ing too slow.

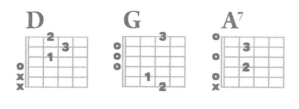

Good night, ladies

2. Farewell, ladies! (3x)
   We're going to leave you now.
   Merrily we roll along,
   roll along, roll along,
   merrily we roll along,
   o'er the deep blue sea.

3. Sweet dreams, ladies! (3x)
   We're going to leave you now.
   Merrily we roll along,
   roll along, roll along,
   merrily we roll along,
   o'er the deep blue sea.

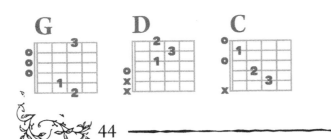

Kum ba yah

2. *Someone's crying, Lord, kum ba yah!*

3. *Someone's singing, Lord, kum ba yah!*

4. *Someone's praying, Lord, kum ba yah!*

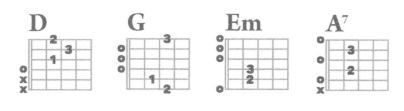

Old black Joe

2. Why do I weep when my heart should feel no pain?
   Why do I sigh that my friends come not again?
   Grieving for forms now departed long ago,
   I hear their gentle voices calling, "Old Black Joe."

3. Where are the hearts once so happy and so free?
   The children so dear that I held upon my knee?
   Gone to the shore where my soul has longed to go,
   I hear their gentle voices calling, "Old Black Joe."

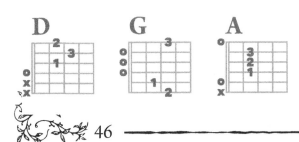

House of the Rising sun

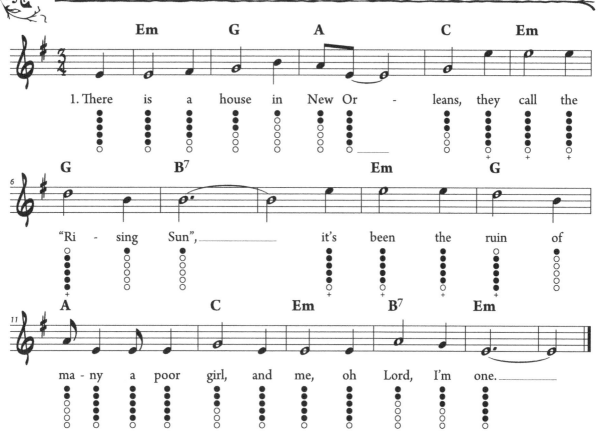

1. There is a house in New Or - leans, they call the
"Ri - sing Sun", it's been the ruin of
ma - ny a poor girl, and me, oh Lord, I'm one.

2. If I had listened what Mamma said,
   I'd been at home today.
   Being so young and foolish, poor boy,
   let a rambler lead me astray.

3. Go tell my baby sister,
   never do like I have done,
   to shun that house in New Orleans,
   they call the Rising Sun.

4. My mother she's a tailor;
   She sold those new blue jeans.
   My sweetheart, he's a drunkard, Lord,
   drinks down in New Orleans.

5. The only thing a drunkard needs,
   is a suitcase and a trunk.

The only time he's satisfied,
is when he's on a drunk.

6. Fills his glasses to the brim,
   passes them around.
   Only pleasure he gets out of life,
   is hoboin' from town to town.

7. One foot is on the platform,
   and the other one on the train.
   I'm going back to New Orleans,
   to wear that ball and chain.

8. Going back to New Orleans,
   my race is almost run.
   Going back to spend the rest of my life,
   beneath that Rising Sun.

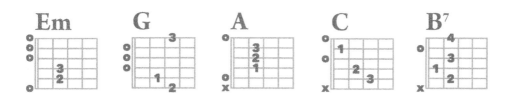

Banks of Sacramento

A bull-y ship and a bull-y-crew, Doo-da! Doo-da! A bull-y mate and a cap-tain, too, Doo-da! Doo-da-day! Then blow, ye winds, hi-oh, for Cal-i-forn-i-o, there's plent-y of gold, so I've been told, on the banks of Sac-ra-men-to!

2. Oh, heave, my lads, oh heave and sing,
   oh, heave and make those oak sticks sing.

3. Our money gone, we shipped to go,
   around Cape Horn, through ice and snow.

4. Oh, around the Horn with a mainskys'l set,
   around Cape Horn and we're all wringin' wet.

5. Around Cape Horn in the month of May,
   with storm winds blowing every day.

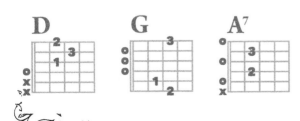

He's got the whole world

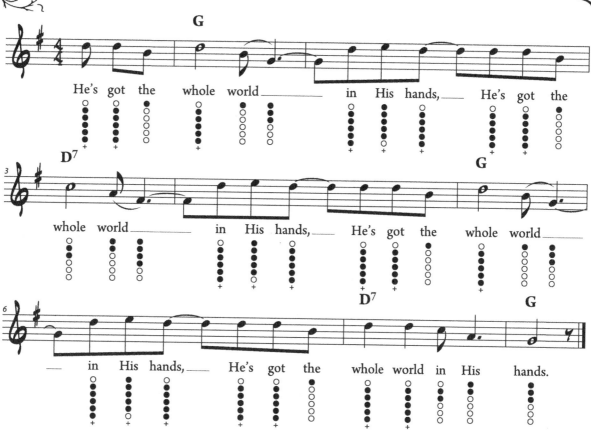

2. *He's got the tiny little baby in His hands.*
3. *He's got you and me brother in His hands.*
4. *He's got the son and the father in His hands.*
5. *He's got the mother and her daughter in His hands.*
6. *He's got everybody here in His hands.*
7. *He's got the sun and the moon in His hands.*
8. *He's got the whole world in his Hands.*

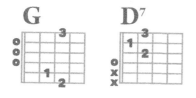

Jingle Bells

2. A day or two ago I thought I'd take a ride,
   and soon Miss Fannie Bright was seated by my side.
   The horse was lean and lank, misfortune seemed his lot,
   he got into a drifted bank and we got upsot.

3. A day or two ago, the story I must tell.
   I went out on the snow, and on my back I fell;
   A gent was riding by in a one-horse open sleigh,
   he laughed as there I sprawling lie, But quickly drove away.

4. Now the ground is white, go it while you're young,
   take the girls tonight and sing this sleighing song.
   Just get a bobtailed bay, two-forty for his speed,
   then hitch him to an open sleigh, and crack! You'll take the lead.

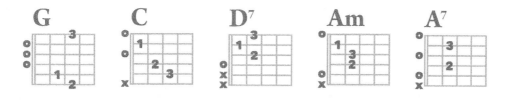

Polly put the kettle on

Pol - ly, put the ket - tle on, Pol - ly, put the ket - le on,

Pol - ly, put the ket - tle on, we'll all have tea.

Su - key, take it off a - gain. Su - key, take it off a - gain,

Su - key, take it off a - gain, they've all gone a - way.

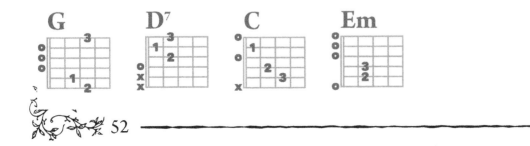

Twinkle, twinkle, little star

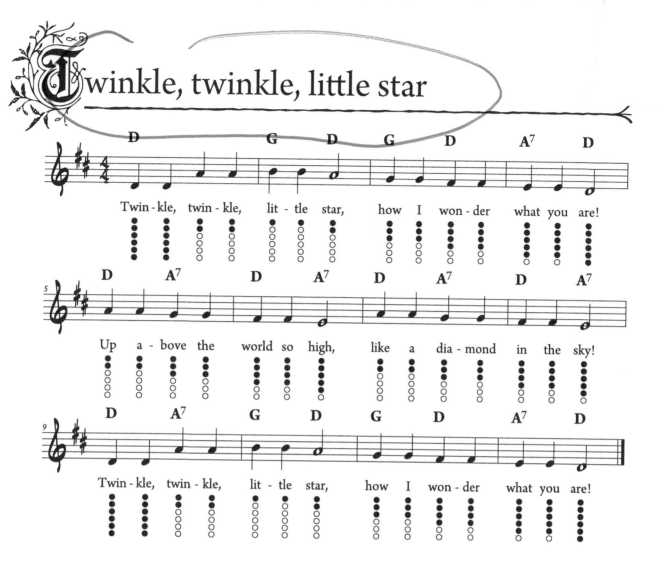

2. When the blazing sun is gone,
   when he nothing shines upon,
   then you show your little light,
   twinkle, twinkle, all the night.

3. Then the traveller in the dark,
   thanks you for your tiny spark,
   he could not see which way to go,
   if you did not twinkle so.

4. In the dark blue sky you keep,
   and often through my curtains peep,
   for you never shut your eye,
   till the sun is in the sky.

5. As your bright and tiny spark,
   lights the traveller in the dark,
   though I know not what you are,
   twinkle, twinkle, little star.

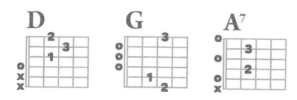

The yellow rose of Texas

C

1. There's a yel - low rose in Tex - as, I'm go - ing there to see. No

D⁷ G G⁷ C

oth - er fel - low loves her, no - bod - y else but me. She cried so when I

G⁷

left her it near - ly broke my heart. And if we ev - er

C G⁷ C

meet a - gain, we nev - er more will part. She's the sweet-est rose of col - or a

G D⁷

fel - ler ev - er knew. Her eyes are bright as dia - monds, they spark-le like the

G G⁷ C

dew. You may talk a - bout your dear-est maids and sing of Ros - a - lie, but the

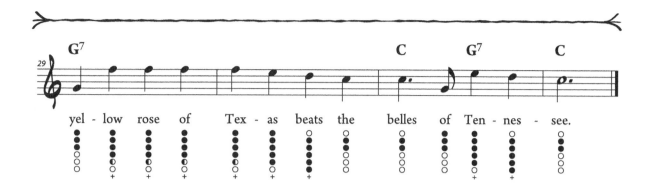

yel - low rose of Tex - as beats the belles of Ten - nes - see.

Chorus:
She's the sweetest rose of color this darky ever knew,
her eyes are bright as diamonds, they sparkle like the dew;
You may talk about your Dearest May, and sing of Rosa Lee,
but the Yellow Rose of Texas is the only girl for me.

2. *When the Rio Grande is flowing, the starry skies are bright,*
   she walks along the river in the quite summer night:
   She thinks if I remember, when we parted long ago,
   I promised to come back again, and not to leave her so.

3. *Oh now I'm going to find her, for my heart is full of woe,*
   and we'll sing the songs togeather, that we sung so long ago
   we'll play the bango gaily, and we'll sing the songs of yore,
   and the Yellow Rose of Texas shall be mine forevermore.

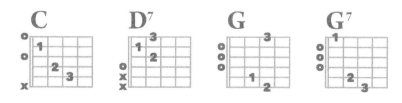

Bound for the Rio Grande

2. So it's pack up your sea-chest an' get underway,
   the girls we are leavin' can have our half-pay.

3. Our ship went sailin' over the bar,
   we've pointed her bow to the southern stars.

4. You Liverpool judies, we'll have you to know,
   we're bound to the south'ard and glad for to go.

5. We're a Liverpool ship & a Liverpool crew,
   you can stick to the coast but I'm damned if we do!

6. Goodbye to Ellen & Molly & Sue,
   you park lane judies, it's goodbye to you.

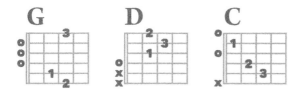

Cindy

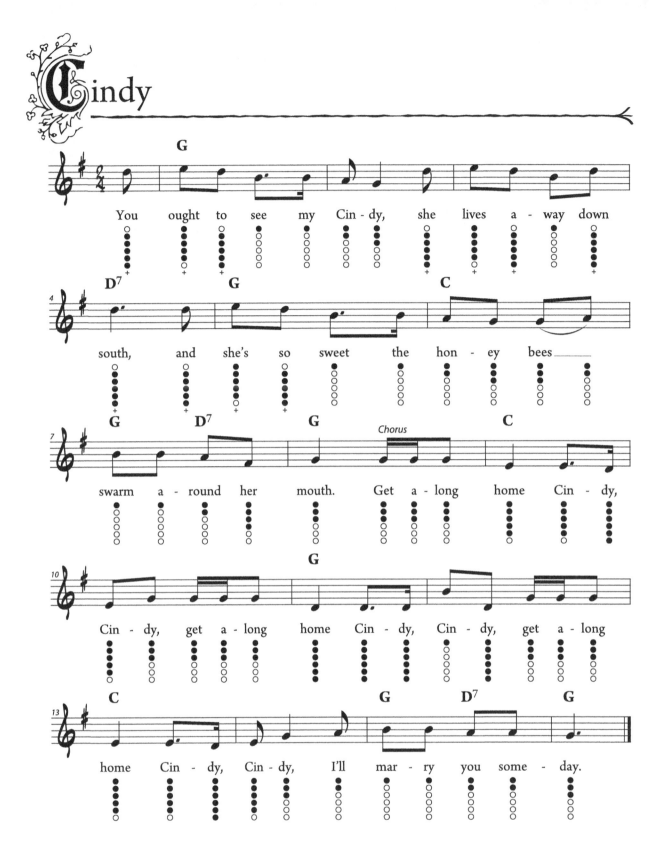

2. The first I seen my Cindy she was standing in the door,
   her shoes and stocking in her hand her feet all over the floor.

3. She took me to her parlor she cooled me with her fan,
   she said I was the prettiest thing in the shape of mortal man.

4. She kissed me and she hugged me she called me suger plum,
   she throwed her arms around me I thought my time had come.

5. Oh Cindy is a pretty girl Cindy is a peach,
   she threw her arms around my neck and hung on like a leech.

6. And if I was a sugar tree standing in the town,
   each time my Cindy passed I'd shake some sugar down.

7. And if had a needle and thread fine as I could sew,
   I'd sew that gal to my coat tails and down the road I'd go.

8. I wish I was an apple a-hanging on a tree,
   every time that Cindy passed she'd take a bite of me.

G 　　**D⁷** 　　**C**

America (My country 'tis of thee)

2. My native country, thee,
   land of the noble free,
   Thy name I love;
   I love thy rocks and rills,
   thy woods and templed hills,
   my heart with rapture thrills
   like that above.

3. Let music swell the breeze,
   and ring from all the trees
   sweet Freedom's song;
   Let mortal tongues awake;
   Let all that breathe partake;
   Let rocks their silence break,
   the sound prolong.

4. Our fathers' God to Thee,
   author of Liberty,
   to thee we sing,
   long may our land be bright
   with Freedom's holy light,
   protect us by thy might
   great God, our King.

5. Our glorious Land to-day,
   'neath Education's sway,
   soars upward still.
   Its hills of learning fair,
   whose bounties all may share,
   behold them everywhere
   on vale and hill!

6. Thy safeguard, Liberty,
   the school shall ever be,
   our Nation's pride!
   No tyrant hand shall smite,
   while with encircling might
   all here are taught the Right
   with Truth allied.

7. Beneath Heaven's gracious will
   the stars of progress still
   our course do sway;
   In unity sublime
   to broader heights we climb,
   triumphant over time,
   God speeds our way!

8. Grand birthright of our sires,
   our altars and our fires
   keep we still pure!
   Our starry flag unfurled,
   the hope of all the world,
   in peace and light impearled,
   God hold secure!

G

Am

D⁷

Em

C

Wayfaring stranger

Em   D   Em   A

1. I am a poor ____ way-far-ing stran-ger, ____ tra-vel-ing through

Em   D

____ this world of woe. ____ And there's no sick ____ ness, toil or

Em   A   Em

dan-ger ____ in that bright land ____ to which I go. ____

Em   D   Bm

____ I'm go-ing there ____ to meet my mo-ther, ____ I'm go-ing

Em   D   B⁷ Em   D

there ____ no more to roam, ____ I'm just a-go - ing o-ver

Em   A   B⁷ Em

Jor-dan, ____ I'm just a-go - ing o-ver home. ____

62

2. I know dark clouds will gather 'round me,
   I know my way is rough and steep.
   Yet golden fields lie just before me,
   where God's redeemed shall ever sleep.
   I'm going there to see my father/mother,
   she/he said he'd/she'd meet me when I come,
   I'm only going over Jordan,
   I'm only going over home.

3. I want to wear a crown of glory,
   when I get home to that good land.
   I want to shout salvation's story
   in concert with the blood-washed band.
   I'm going there to meet my Saviour,
   to sing his praise forever more,
   I'm just a-going over Jordan,
   I'm just a-going over home.

Em   **D**   **A**   **Bm** 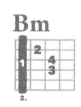   **B⁷**

Will the circle be unbroken

2. I said to the undertaker,
   "Undertaker please drive slow.
   For that body you are carrying,
   Lord, I hate to see her go."

3. Well I followed close behind her,
   tried to hold up and be brave.
   But I could not hide my sorrow,
   when they laid her in that grave.

4. I went back home, Lord, that home was lonesome.
   Since my mother, she was gone,
   all my brothers and sisters crying.
   What a home so sad and alone.

G   **G**⁷   **C**   **D**⁷

Whiskey in the jar

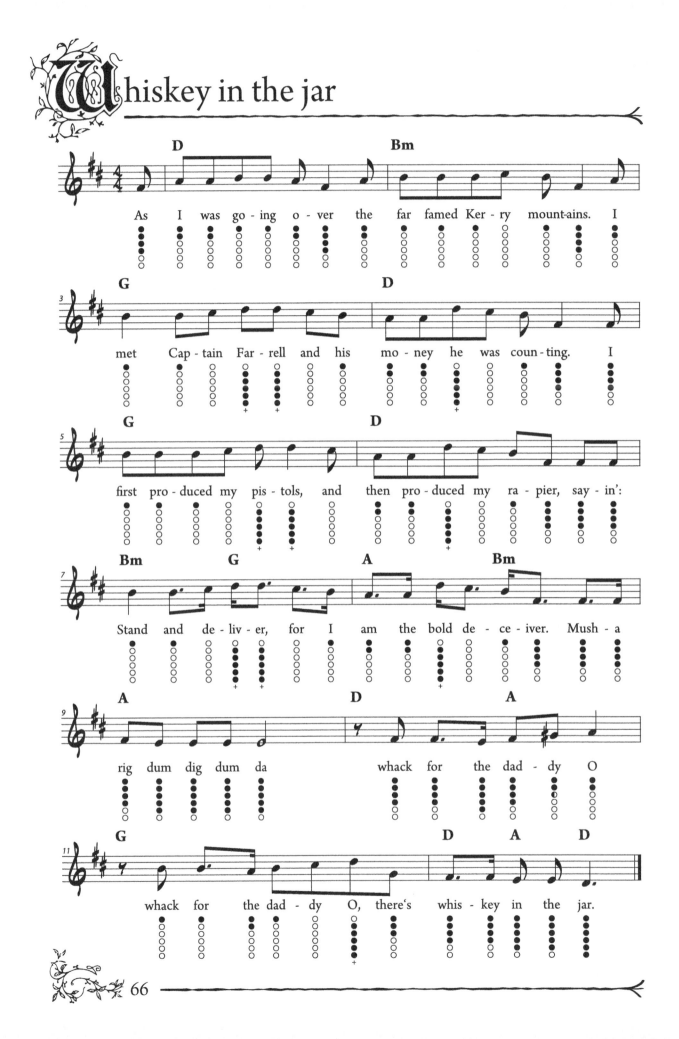

As I was go-ing o-ver the far famed Ker-ry mount-ains. I met Cap-tain Far-rell and his mo-ney he was coun-ting. I first pro-duced my pis-tols, and then pro-duced my ra-pier, say-in': Stand and de-liv-er, for I am the bold de-ce-iver. Mush-a rig dum dig dum da whack for the dad-dy O whack for the dad-dy O, there's whis-key in the jar.

2. I counted out his money, and it made a pretty penny.
   I put it in my pocket and I took it home to Jenny.
   She said and she swore, that she never would deceive me,
   but the devil take the women, for they never can be easy.

3. I went into my chamber, all for to take a slumber,
   I dreamt of gold and jewels and for sure it was no wonder.
   But Jenny took my charges and she filled them up with water,
   Then sent for captain Farrel to be ready for the slaughter.

4. It was early in the morning, as I rose up for travel,
   The guards were all around me and likewise captain Farrel.
   I first produced my pistol, for she stole away my rapier,
   But I couldn't shoot the water so a prisoner I was taken.

5. If anyone can aid me, it's my brother in the army,
   If I can find his station down in Cork or in Killarney.
   And if he'll come and save me, we'll go roving near Kilkenny,
   And I swear he'll treat me better than me darling sportling Jenny.

6. Now some men take delight in the drinking and the roving,
   But others take delight in the gambling and the smoking.
   But I take delight in the juice of the barley,
   And courting pretty fair maids in the morning bright and early.

D   **Bm**   **G**   **A**

Camptown races

2. *De long tail filly and de big black hoss, doo-dah, doo-dah!*
   Dey fly de track and dey both cut across, Oh, doo-dah-day!
   De blind hoss sticken in a big mud hole, doo-dah, doo-dah!
   Can't touch bottom wid a ten foot pole, oh, doo-dah-day!

Refrain

3. *Old muley cow come on to de track, doo-dah, doo-dah!*
   De bob-tail fling her ober his back, oh, doo-dah-day!
   Den fly along like a rail-road car, doo-dah, doo-dah!
   Runnin' a race wid a shootin' star, oh, doo-dah-day!

Refrain

4. *See dem flyin' on a ten mile heat, doo-dah, doo-dah!*
   Round de race track, den repeat, oh, doo-dah-day!
   I win my money on de bob-tail nag, doo-dah, doo-dah!
   I keep my money in an old tow-bag, oh, doo-dah-day!

D   **A**   **G**

arbara Allen

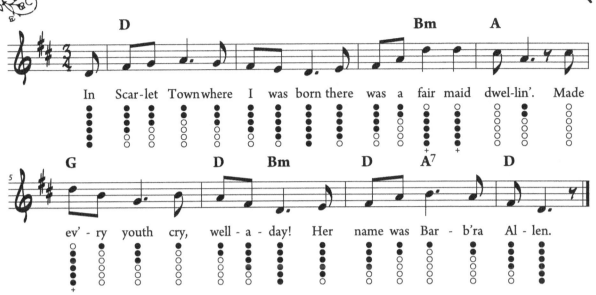

In Scar-let Town where I was born there was a fair maid dwel-lin'. Made
ev' - ry youth cry, well - a - day! Her name was Bar - b'ra Al - len.

2. All in the merry month of May,
   when green leaves they was springing,
   this young man on his death-bed lay,
   for the love of Barbara Allen.

3. He sent his man unto her then,
   to the town where she was dwelling:
   "You must come to my master dear,
   if your name be Barbara Allen."

4. "For death is printed in his face,
   and sorrow's in him dwelling,
   and you must come to my master dear,
   if your name be Barbara Allen."

5. "If death be printed in his face,
   and sorrow's in him dwelling,
   then little better shall he be
   for bonny Barbara Allen."

6. So slowly, slowly she got up,
   and so slowly she came to him,
   and all she said when she came there,
   "Young man, I think you are a dying."

7. He turnd his face unto her then:
   "If you be Barbara Allen."
   "My dear," said he, "come pitty me,
   as on my death-bed I am lying."

8. "If on your death-bed you be lying,
   what is that to Barbara Allen?
   I cannot keep you from [your] death;
   So farewell," said Barbara Allen.

9. He turnd his face unto the wall,
   and death came creeping to him:
   "Then adieu, adieu, and adieu to all,
   and adieu to Barbara Allen!"

10. And as she was walking on a day,
    she heard the bell a ringing,
    and it did seem to ring to her
    "Unworthy Barbara Allen."

11. She turnd herself round about,
    and she spy'd the corps a coming:
    "Lay down, lay down the corps of clay,
    that I may look upon him."

12. While all her friends cry'd amain,
    so loudly she lay laughing,
    while all her friends cry'd amain,
    "Unworthy Barbara Allen!"

13. When he was dead, and laid in grave,
    then death came creeping to she:
    "O mother, mother, make my bed,
    for his death hath quite undone me."

14. "A hard-hearted creature that I was,
    to slight one that lovd me so dearly;
    I wish I had been more kinder to him,
    the time of his life when he was near me."

15. So this maid she then did dye,
    and desired to be buried by him,
    and repented her self before she dy'd,
    that ever she did deny him.

D   **Bm** 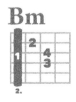 **A**   **G**   **A⁷**

Buffalo gals

1. As I went walk-ing down the street, down the street, down the street, a
pret-ty girl I chanced to meet un-der the sil-ver-y moon.

Chorus
Buf-fa-lo gals, will you come out to-night, come out to-night, come out to-night,
Buf-fa-lo gals, will you come out to-night, and dance by the light of the moon.

2. I asked her would she have some talk,
   have some talk, have some talk.
   Her feet covered the whole sidewalk
   as she stood close by me.

3. I asked her would she have a dance,
   have a dance, have a dance.
   I thought I might get a chance
   to shake a foot with her.

4. I'd like to make that gal my wife,
   gal my wife, gal my wife.
   I'd be happy all my life.
   If I had her by me.

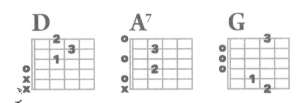

Sailor on the deep blue sea

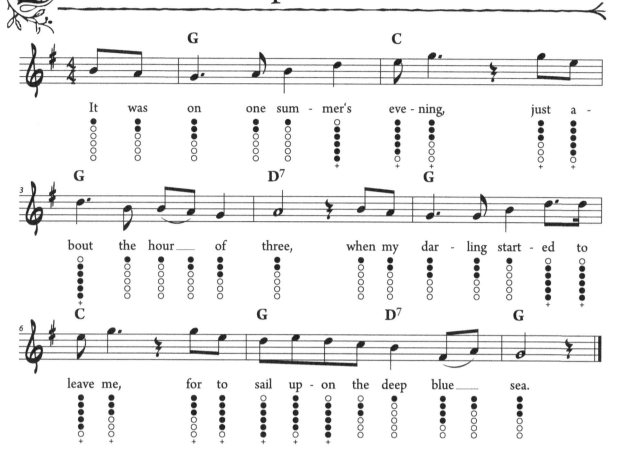

It was on one sum-mer's eve-ning, just a-bout the hour ___ of three, when my dar-ling start-ed to leave me, for to sail up-on the deep blue ___ sea.

2. Oh, he promised to write me a letter,
   he said he'd write to me;
   But I've not heard from my darling
   who is sailing on the deep blue sea.

3. Oh, my mother's dead and buried,
   my pa's forsaken me,
   and I have no one for to love me
   but the sailor on the deep blue sea.

4. Oh captain, can you tell me
   where can my sailor be;
   Oh yes, my little maiden,
   he is drownded in the deep blue sea.

5. Farewell to friends and relations,
   it's the last you'll see of me;
   For I'm going to end my troubles
   by drowning in the deep blue sea.

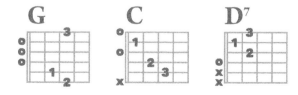

The Wabash Cannon Ball

Chorus:
Listen to the jingle, the rumble and the roar
as she glides along the woodland, through the hills and by the shore.
Hear the mighty rush of the engine, hear that lonesome hobo squall.
You're travelling through the jungles on the Wabash Cannonball.

2. *She came down from Birmingham, one cold December day,*
   as she rolled into the station, you could hear all the people say,
   "There's a girl from Tennessee, she's long and she's tall
   She came down from Birmingham on the Wabash Cannonball."

3. *Our the Eastern states are dandy so the people always say,*
   "From New York to St. Louis and Chicago by the way
   from the hills of Minnesota where the rippling waters fall,
   no changes can be taken on that Wabash Cannonball."

4. *Here's to daddy Claxton, may his name forever stand*
   and always be remembered 'round the courts of Alabam'.
   His earthly race is over and the curtains 'round him fall.
   We'll carry him home to victory on the Wabash Cannonball.

Greensleeves

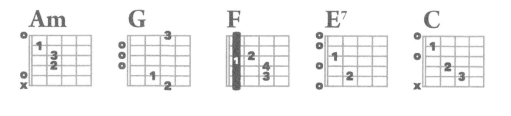

John Brown's body

2. He's gone to be a soldier in the Army of the Lord, (3x)
His soul goes marching on.

Chorus:
Glory, glory, hallelujah, (3x)
His soul goes marching on.

3. John Brown's knapsack is strapped upon his back, (3x)
His soul goes marching on.

Chorus

4. John Brown died that the slaves might be free, (3x)
His soul goes marching on.

Chorus

5. The stars above in Heaven now are looking kindly down, (3x)
His soul goes marching on.

Chorus

C   **F**   **Am**   **Dm**   **G**[7]

My Bonnie lies over the ocean

2. Last night as I lay on my pillow,
    last night as I lay on my bed.
    Last night as I lay on my pillow,
    I dreamed that my Bonnie was dead.
    Bring back, bring back,
    bring back my Bonnie to me, to me.
    Bring back, bring back,
    bring back my Bonnie to me.

3. Oh blow ye the winds o'er the ocean,
    and blow ye the winds o'er the sea.
    Oh blow ye the winds o'er the ocean,
    and bring back my Bonnie to me.
    Bring back, bring back,
    bring back my Bonnie to me, to me.
    Bring back, bring back,
    bring back my Bonnie to me.

4. The winds have blown over the ocean,
    the winds have blown over the sea.
    The winds have blown over the ocean,
    and brought back my Bonnie to me.
    Bring back, bring back,
    bring back my Bonnie to me, to me.
    Bring back, bring back,
    bring back my Bonnie to me.

Old folks at home

2. All 'round the little farm I wandered,
   when I was young.
   Then many happy days I squandered,
   many the songs I sung,
   when I was playing with my brother,
   happy was I.
   Oh, take me to my kind old mother,
   there let me live and die.

3. One little hut among the bushes,
   one that I love,
   still sadly to my mem'ry rushes,
   no matter where I rove,
   when shall I see the bees a-humming,
   all 'round the comb,
   when shall I hear the banjo strumming,
   down by my good old home.

D   **A⁷**   **G**   **E⁷**

Billy Boy

2. Did she bid you to come in, Billy Boy, Billy Boy?
   Did she bid you to come in, charming Billy?
   Yes, she bade me to come in, there's a dimple in her chin.
   She's a young thing and cannot leave her mother.

3. Can she make a cherry pie, Billy Boy, Billy Boy?
   Can she make a cherry pie, charming Billy?
   She can make a cherry pie, quick as a cat can wink an eye,
   she's a young thing and cannot leave her mother.

4. Did she set for you a chair, Billy Boy, Billy Boy?
   Did she set for you a chair, charming Billy?
   Yes, she sat for me a chair, she has ringlets in her hair.
   She's a young thing and cannot leave her mother.

5. How old is she now, Billy Boy, Billy Boy?
   How old is she now, charming Billy?
   Three times six and four times seven, twenty-eight and eleven,
   she's a young thing and cannot leave her mother.

G **D⁷** **Em** **A⁷** **C**

The wild rover

2. I went to an alehouse I used to frequent,
   and I told the landlady me money was spent.
   I asked her for credit, she answered me "nay,
   such a custom as yours I could have any day".

3. I pulled from me pocket a handful of gold,
   and on the round table it glittered and rolled.
   She said "I have whiskeys and wines of the best,
   and the words that I told you were only in jest".

4. I'll have none of your whiskeys nor fine Spanish wines,
   for your words show you clearly as no friend of mine.
   There's others most willing to open a door,
   To a man coming home from a far distant shore.

5. I'll go home to me parents, confess what I've done,
   and I'll ask them to pardon their prodigal son.
   And if they forgive me as oft times before,
   I never will play the wild rover no more.

What shall we do with the drunken sailor

2. Give him a dose of salent water, early ...
3. Give him a dash with a besoms rubber, early ...
4. Pull out the plug and wet him all over, early ...
5. Heave him by the leg in a running bowlin', early ...
6. That's what to do with a drunken sailor, early ...

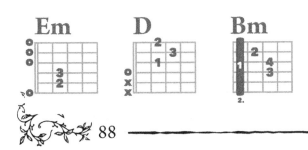

Skip to my lou

G

Fly's in the but-ter-milk, shoo, fly, shoo. Fly's in the but-ter-milk,

G

Shoo, fly, shoo. Fly's in the but-ter-milk, shoo, fly, shoo.

D   G   D

Skip to my Lou, my dar-ling. Skip, skip, skip to my Lou, skip, skip,

G   D   G

skip to my Lou, skip, skip, skip to my Lou, skip to my Lou, my dar-ling.

2. There's a little red wagon, paint it blue

3. Lost my partner, what'll I do?

4. I'll get another one, prettier than you

5. Can't get a red bird, jaybird'll do

6. Cat's in the cream jar, ooh, ooh, ooh

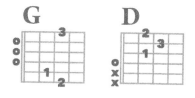

G   D

Scarborough Fair

2. Tell her to make me a cambric shirt,
   parsley, sage, rosemary, and thyme;
   Without a seam or needlework,
   then she shall be a true lover of mine.

3. Tell her to wash it in yonder well,
   parsley, sage, rosemary, and thyme;
   where never spring water or rain ever fell,
   and she shall be a true lover of mine.

4. Tell her to dry it on yonder thorn,
   parsley, sage, rosemary, and thyme;
   Which never bore blossom since Adam was born,
   then she shall be a true lover of mine.

5. Now he has asked me questions three,
   parsley, sage, rosemary, and thyme;
   I hope he'll answer as many for me
   before he shall be a true lover of mine.

6. Tell him to buy me an acre of land,
   parsley, sage, rosemary, and thyme;
   Between the salt water and the sea sand,
   then he shall be a true lover of mine.

7. Tell him to plough it with a ram's horn,
   parsley, sage, rosemary, and thyme;
   And sow it all over with one pepper corn,
   and he shall be a true lover of mine.

8. Tell him to sheer't with a sickle of leather,
   parsley, sage, rosemary, and thyme;
   And bind it up with a peacock feather.
   And he shall be a true lover of mine.

9. Tell him to thrash it on yonder wall,
   parsley, sage, rosemary, and thyme,
   and never let one corn of it fall,
   then he shall be a true lover of mine.

10. When he has done and finished his work.
    Parsley, sage, rosemary, and thyme:
    Oh, tell him to come and he'll have his shirt,
    and he shall be a true lover of mine.

Em **D** **G** **A** **C**

She'll be comin' round the mountain

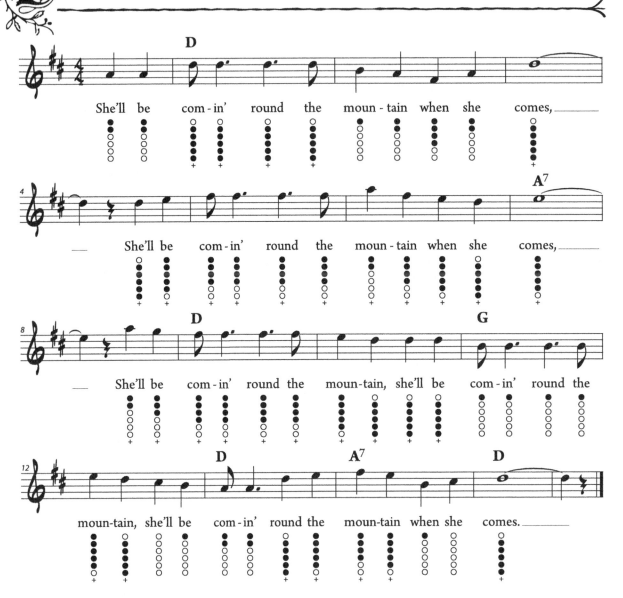

2. She'll be drivin' six white horses when she comes ...
3. We will all go out to meet her when she comes ...
4. We will have chickden an' dumplin's when she comes ...
5. She'll be reelin' an' a-rockin' when she comes ...
6. We'll shout glory hallelujah when she comes ...

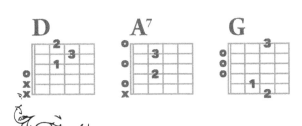

Shenandoah

2. Oh Shenandoah,
   I love your daughter,
   away, you rolling river.
   For her I'd cross,
   your roaming waters,
   away, I'm bound away,
   'cross the wide Missouri.

3. 'Tis seven years,
   since last I've seen you,
   away, you rolling river.
   'Tis seven years,
   since last I've seen you,
   away, we're bound away,
   'cross the wide Missouri.

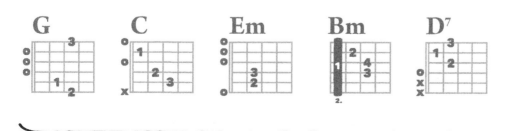

Down by the riverside

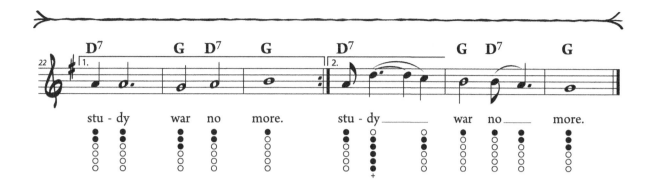

2. I'm goin' to lay down my sword and shield ...

3. I'm goin' to put on my travelin' shoes ...

4. I'm goin' to put on my starry crown ...

5. Gonna put on my golden shoes ...

6. Gonna talk with the Prince of Peace ...

7. Gonna shake hands around the world ...

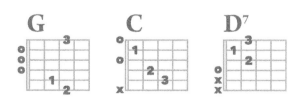

Swing low, sweet chariot

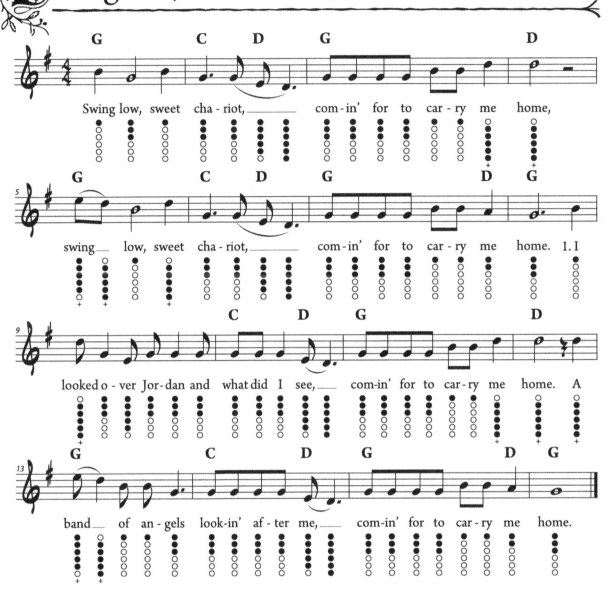

2. If you get there before I do,
   comin' for to carry me home,
   tell all o' God's children that I'm comin' too,
   comin' for to carry me home.

3. I'm sometimes up, I'm sometimes down,
   comin' for to carry me home,
   but still my soul feels heavenly bound,
   comin' for to carry me home.

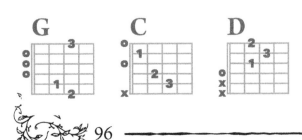

Up on the housetop

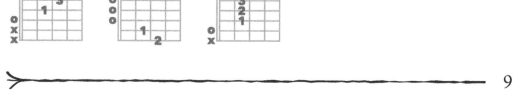

Go, tell it on the mountain

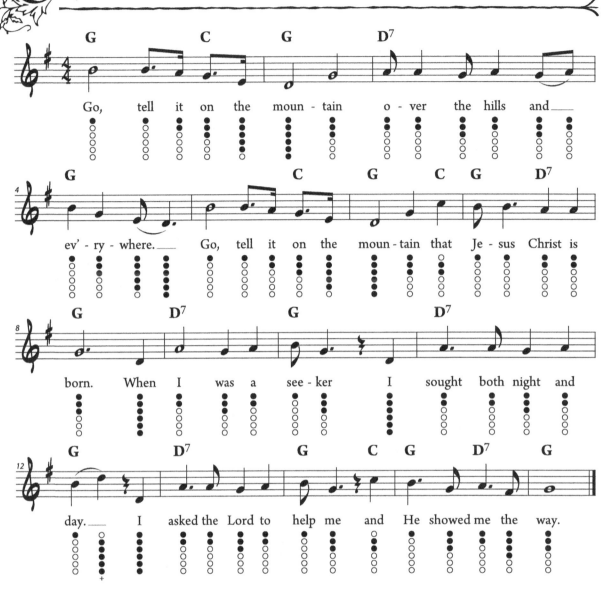

Go, tell it on the moun-tain o-ver the hills and ev'-ry-where. Go, tell it on the moun-tain that Je-sus Christ is born. When I was a see-ker I sought both night and day. I asked the Lord to help me and He showed me the way.

2. He made me a watchman upon the city wall,
   and if I am a Christian I am the least of all.

3. 'Twas a lowly manger that Jesus Christ was born.
   The Lord sent down an angel that bright and glorious morn'.

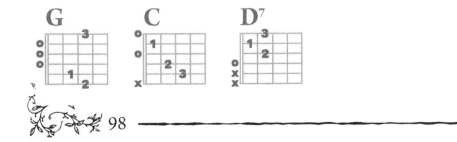

I'm on my way

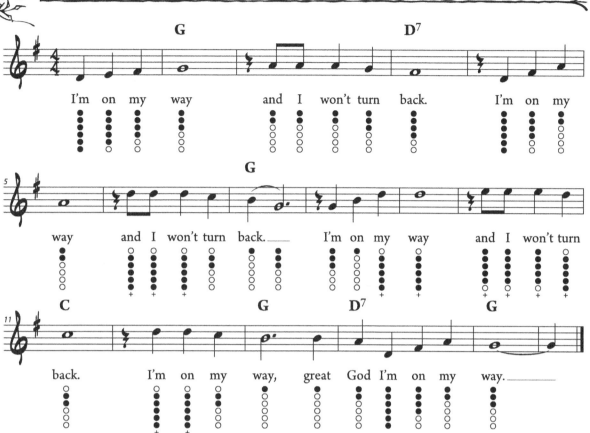

Lyrics under the music: I'm on my way and I won't turn back. I'm on my way and I won't turn back. I'm on my way and I won't turn back. I'm on my way, great God I'm on my way.

2. I'll ask my brother, come, go with me. (3x)
   I'm on my way, great God, I'm on my way.

3. If he won't come, I'll go alone. (3x)
   I'm on my way, great God, I'm on my way.

4. I'll ask my sister, come, go with me. (3x)
   I'm on my way, great God, I'm on my way.

5. If she won't come, I'll go anyhow. (3x)
   I'm on my way, great God, I'm on my way.

6. I'm on my way to the freedom land. (3x)
   I'm on my way, great God, I'm on my way.

7. I'm on my way and I won't turn back. (3x)
   I'm on my way, great God, I'm on my way.

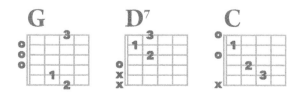

ℒittle brown jug

2. *When I go toiling on the farm*
   I take the little jug under my arm;
   Place it under a shady tree,
   little brown jug, 'tis you and me.

3. *'Tis you that makes me friends and foes,*
   'tis you that makes me wear old clothes;
   But, seeing you're so near my nose,
   tip her up and down she goes.

4. *If all the folks in Adam's race*
   were gathered together in one place,
   I'd let them go without a tear
   before I'd part from you, my dear.

5. *If I'd a cow that gave such milk,*
   I'd dress her in the finest silk;
   Feed her up on oats and hay,
   and milk her twenty times a day.

6. *I bought a cow from Farmer Jones,*
   and she was nothing but skin and bones;
   I fed her up as fine as silk,
   she jumped the fence and strained her milk.

7. *And when I die don't bury me at all,*
   just pickle my bones in alcohol;
   Put a bottle o' booze at my head and feet
   and then I know that I will keep.

8. *The rose is red, my nose is too,*
   the violet's blue and so are you;
   And yet, I guess, before I stop,
   we'd better take another drop.

Nobody knows the trouble I've seen

2. Although you see me going 'long so,
   oh, yes, Lord.
   I have my trials here below,
   oh, yes, Lord.
   If you get there before I do,
   oh, yes, Lord.
   Tell all-a my friends I'm coming too,
   oh, yes, Lord.

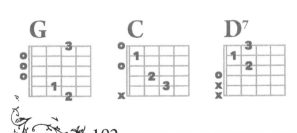

Oh! Susannah

I — came from A - la - ba - ma with my — ban - jo on my knee, I'm — goin' to Lou' - si - a - na, my Su - san - na for to see. Oh! Su - san - na, oh don't you cry for me, for I come from A - la - ba - ma with my — ban - jo on my knee.

2. I had a dream the other night
when ev'rything was still;
I thought I saw Susanna
a-comin' down the hill;
the buckwheat cake was in her mouth,
the tear was in her eye;
says I, I'm comin' from the south,
Susanna, don't you cry.
Oh! Susanna,
oh, don't you cry for me ...

3. I soon will be in New Orleans,
and then I'll look around,
and when I find Susanna
I'll fall upon the ground.
And if I do not find her,
then I will surely die,
and when I'm dead and buried,
Susanna, don't you cry.
Oh! Susanna,
oh, don't you cry for me ...

D

A⁷

G

Michael, row the boat ashore

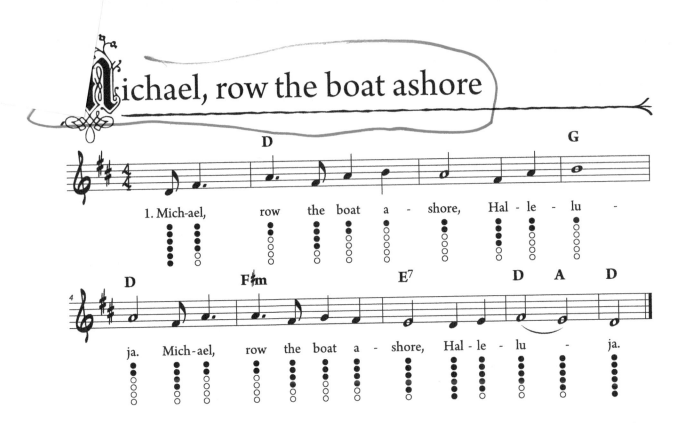

1. Mich-ael, row the boat a - shore, Hal - le - lu - ja. Mich-ael, row the boat a - shore, Hal - le - lu - ja.

2. Michael boat a gospelboat, Halleluja ...

3. Brother lend a helping hand, Halleluja ...

4. Sister help to trim the sail, Halleluja ...

5. Boasting talk will sink your soul, Halleluja ...

6. Jordan-stream is deep and wide, Halleluja ...

7. Jesus stand on the other side, Halleluja ...

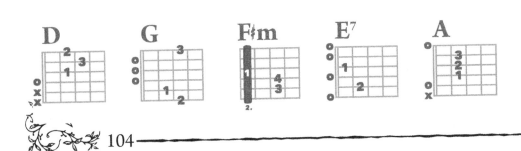

Morning has broken

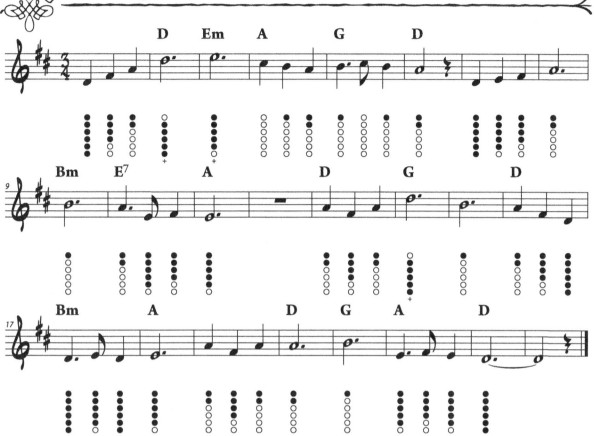

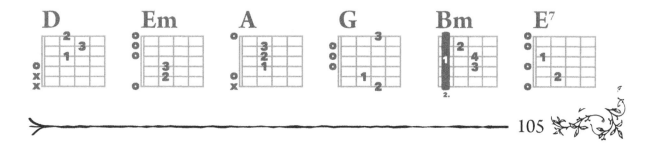

Joshua fit the battle

2. *Right up to the walls of Jericho.*
   He marched with spear in Hand.
   Go, blow dat ram's horn, Joshua cried,
   'cause de battle am in my hand.

3. *Then de lamb ram sheep horns begin a blow.*
   Trumpets begin to sound.
   Joshua commanded de children to shout,
   and de walls came tumbling down.
   Joshua fit de battle of Jericho ...

Jolly good fellow

For he's a jol - ly good fel - low, for he's a jol - ly good fel - low, for he's a jol - ly good fel - low, which no - bo - dy can de - ny!

2. We won't go home until morning, (3x)
   'till daylight doth appear.
   'Till daylight doth appear,
   'till daylight doth appear.
   We won't go home until morning, (3x)
   'till daylight doth appear.

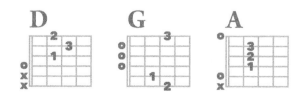

Home on the range

2. *How often at night, when the heavens are bright*
   with the light from the glittering stars,
   have I stood there amazed and I asked as I gazed,
   if their glory exceeds that of ours.
   Home, home ...

3. *Where the air is so pure and the zephyrs so free*
   and the breezes so balmy and light,
   that I would not exchange my home on the range
   for all the cities so bright.
   Home, home ...

Home! Sweet home

2. *An exile from home, spendor dazzles in vain,*
   oh, give me my lowly thatched cottage again;
   The birds singing gaily, that come at my call;
   Give me them, with that peace of mind, dearer than all.

3. *To thee, I'll return, overburdened with care,*
   the heart's dearest solace will smile on me there.
   No more from that cottage again will I roam,
   be it ever so humble, there's no place like home.

D

G

A⁷

Em

The last rose of summer

2. I'll not leave thee, thou lone one!
   To pine on the stem;
   Since the lovely are sleeping,
   go, sleep thou with them.
   Thus kindly I scatter,
   thy leaves o'er the bed,
   where thy mates of the garden
   lie scentless and dead.

3. So soon may I follow,
   when friendships decay,
   and from Love's shining circle
   the gems drop away.
   When true hearts lie withered,
   and fond ones are flown.
   Oh! who would inhabit
   this bleak world alone?

D   **G**   **A** 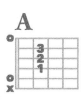   **Bm**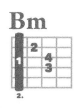

The ballad of John Henry

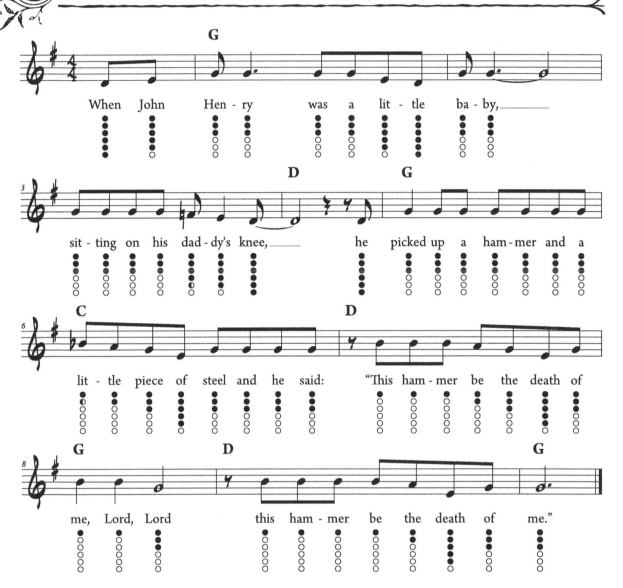

2. The captain said to John Henry:
"Gonna bring that steam drill 'round,
gonna bring that sterm drill out on the job,
gonna whop that steel on down, Lord, Lord,
gonna whop that steel on down."

3. John Henry told his captain:
"A man ain't nothing but a man,
nut before I let your steam drill beat me down,
I'd die with a hammer in my hand, Lord, Lord,
I'd die with a hammer in my hand."

4. John Henry said to his shaker:
"Shaker, why don't you sing?
I'm throwin' thirty pounds from my hips on down,
just listen to that cold steel ring, Lord, Lord,
just listen to that cold steel ring."

5. John Henry said to his shaker:
"Shaker, you'd better pray,
'cause if I miss that little piece of steel,
tomorrow be your buryin' day, Lord, Lord,
tomorrow be your buryin' day."

6. The shaker said to John Henry:
   "I think this mountain's cavin' in!"
   John Henry said to his shaker, "Man,
   that ain't nothin' but my hammer suckin' wind! Lord, Lord,
   that ain't nothin' but my hammer suckin' wind!"

7. Now the man that invented the steam drill,
   thought he was mighty fine.
   But John Henry made fifteen feet,
   the steam drill only made nine, Lord, Lord,
   the steam drill only made nine.

8. John Henry hammered in the mountains,
   his hammer was striking fire.
   But he worked so hard, he broke his poor heart,
   he laid down his hammer and he died, Lord, Lord,
   he laid down his hammer and he died.

9. John Henry had a little woman,
   her name was Polly Ann.
   John Henry took sick and went to his bed,
   Polly Ann drove steel like a man, Lord, Lord,
   Polly Ann drove steel like a man.

10. John Henry had a little baby,
    you could hold him in the palm of your hand.
    The last words I heard that poor boy say:
    "My daddy was a steel driving man, Lord, Lord,
    my daddy was a steel driving man."

11. They took John Henry to the graveyard,
    and they buried him in the sand.
    And every locomotive comes a-roaring by
    says "There lies a steel-driving man, Lord, Lord,
    there lies a steel-driving man."

12. Well every Monday morning,
    when the bluebirds begin to sing,
    you can hear John Henry a mile or more,
    you can hear John Henry's hammer ring, Lord, Lord,
    you can hear John Henry's hammer ring.

Softly and tenderly

2. *Why should we tarry when Jesus is pleading,*
   pleading for you and for me.
   Why should we linger and heed not His mercies,
   mercies for you and for me.

3. *Time is now fleeting, the moments are passing,*
   passing for you and for me.
   Shadows are gathering, death's night is coming,
   coming for you and for me.

4. *O for the wonderful love He has promised,*
   promised for you and for me!
   Though we have sinned, He has mercy and pardon,
   pardon for you and for me.

G **C** **Em** **A** **D** **E**

Reilly's daughter

As I was sit-ting by the fire, tal-king to old Reil-ly's daugh-ter sud-den-ly a thought came in-to my head: I'd like to mar-ry old Reil-ly's daugh-ter, gid-dy-I-ay, gid-dy-I-ay, gid-dy-I-ay for the one-eyed Reil-ly, gid-dy-I-ay (bang, bang, bang), play it on your big bass drum!

2. Reilly played on the big bass drum.
   Reilly had a mind for murder and slaughter.
   Reilly had a bright red glittering eye
   and he kept that eye on his lovely daughter.
   Giddy i-ae, Giddy i-ae ...

3. Her hair was black and her eyes were blue.
   The colonel and the major and the captain sought her.
   The sergeant and the private and the drummer boy too.
   But they never had a chance with Reilly's daughter.
   Giddy i-ae, Giddy i-ae ...

4. I got me a ring and a parson, too.
   Got me a scratch in a married quarter.
   Settled me down to a peaceful life,
   happy as a king with Reilly's daughter.
   Giddy i-ae, Giddy i-ae ...

5. Suddenly a footstep on the stairs
   who should it be but Reilly out for slaughter.
   With two pistols in his hands
   looking for the man who had married his daughter.
   Giddy i-ae, Giddy i-ae ...

6. I caught O'Reilly by the hair,
   rammed his head in a pail of water.
   Fired his pistols into the air,
   a damned sight quicker than I married his daughter.
   Giddy i-ae, Giddy i-ae ...

A **E⁷**

Poor Paddy works on the railway

2. In eighteen hundred and forty-two
   I didn't know what I should do.
   I didn't know what I should do,
   to work upon the railway, the railway,
   I'm weary of the railway,
   poor Paddy works on the railway.

3. In eighteen hundred and forty-three
   I sailed away across the sea.
   I sailed away across the sea,
   to work upon the railway, the railway,
   I'm weary of the railway,
   poor Paddy works on the railway

4. In eighteen hundred and forty-four
   I landed on Columbia's shore.
   I landed on Columbia's shore,
   to work upon the railway, the railway.
   I'm weary of the railway,
   poor Paddy works on the railway.

5. In eighteen hundred and forty-five
   when Daniel O'Connell he was alive.
   When Daniel O'Connell he was alive
   to work upon the railway, the railway.
   I'm weary of the railway,
   poor Paddy works on the railway.

6. In eighteen hundred and forty-six
   I made my trade to carrying bricks.
   I made my trade to carrying bricks
   for working on the railway.
   I'm weary of the railway,
   poor Paddy works on the railway.

7. In eighteen hundred and forty-seven
   poor Paddy was thinking of going to Heaven.
   poor Paddy was thinking of going to Heaven,
   to work upon the railway, the railway.
   I'm weary of the railway,
   poor Paddy works on the railway.

Am **F** **G** **Em** **C**

God rest ye merry, gentlemen

2. In Bethlehem, in Israel,
   this blessed Babe was born,
   and laid within a manger
   upon this blessed morn,
   the which His Mother Mary
   did nothing take in scorn:
   O tidings ...

3. From God our heavenly Father
   a blessed angel came,
   and unto certain shepherds
   brought tidings of the same,
   how that in Bethlehem was born
   the Son of God by name:
   O tidings ...

4. The shepherds at those tidings
   rejoicèd much in mind,
   and left their flocks a-feeding
   in tempest, storm and wind,
   and went to Bethlehem straightway,
   this blessèd Babe to find:
   O tidings ...

5. But when to Bethlehem they came,
   whereat this Infant lay,
   they found Him in a manger,
   where oxen feed on hay;
   His mother Mary kneeling,
   unto the Lord did pray:
   O tidings ...

6. Now to the Lord sing praises,
   all you within this place,
   and with true love and brotherhood
   each other now embrace;
   This holy tide of Christmas
   all others doth deface:
   O tidings ...

Em B C G D

Hard times come again no more

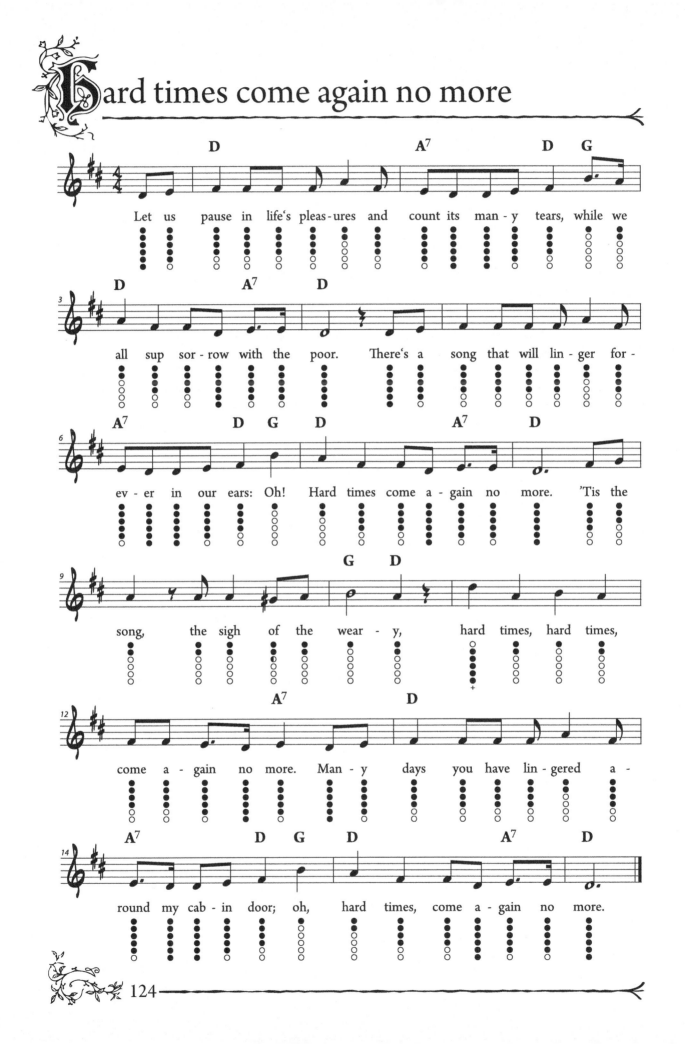

2. While we seek mirth and beauty and music light and gay,
    there are frail forms fainting at the door;
    Though their voices are silent, their pleading looks will say
    Oh! Hard times come again no more.
    'Tis the song, the sigh of the weary ...

3. There's a pale drooping maiden who toils her life away,
    with a worn heart whose better days are o'er:
    Though her voice would be merry, ,tis sighing all the day,
    Oh! Hard times come again no more.
    'Tis the song, the sigh of the weary ...

4. 'Tis a sigh that is wafted across the troubled wave,
    'tis a wail that is heard upon the shore,
    'tis a dirge that is murmured around the lowly grave
    Oh! Hard times come again no more.
    'Tis the song, the sigh of the weary ...

Old MacDonald

Old Mac Do - nald had a farm, E I E I O! And

on his farm he had some chicks, E I E I O! With a

chick - chick here and a chick-chick there. Here a chick, there a chick,

ev - ry - where a chick - chick. Old Mac Do - nald had a farm, E I E I O!

2. ... he had some geese ...
   With a gabble-gabble here ...

3. ... he had a pig ...
   With an oinck-oink here ...

4. ... he had some ducks ...
   With a quack-quack here ...

5. ... he had a cow ...
   With a moo-moo here ...

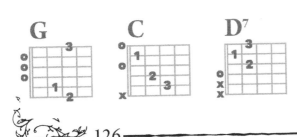

Over the river and through the woods

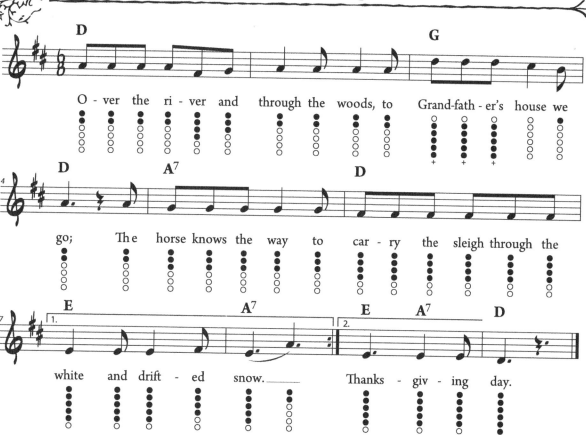

O - ver the ri - ver and through the woods, to Grand-fath - er's house we go; The horse knows the way to car - ry the sleigh through the white and drift - ed snow._____ Thanks - giv - ing day.

2. Over the river and through the woods,
   to have a first-rate play;
   Oh, hear the bells ring, "Ting-a-ling-ling!"
   Hurrah for Thanksgiving Day!
   Over the river and through the woods,
   trot fast, my dapple gray!
   Spring over the ground, Like a hunting hound!
   For this is Thanksgiving Day.

3. Over the river and through the woods,
   and straight through the barnyard gate.
   We seem to go extremely slow
   it is so hard to wait!
   Over the river and through the woods,
   now Grandmother's cap I spy!
   Hurrah for the fun! Is the pudding done?
   Hurrah for the pumpkin pie!

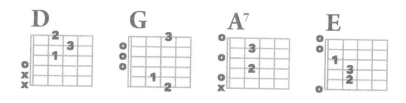

ingering chart for tin whistle

O = open hole   ● = closed hole   ◖ = half-closed hole   + = overblowing

Ornaments

Ornaments play an important role in traditional Irish music. When and how to use them is most often left to the musicians' taste and discretion. The following is a brief outline of the most common ornaments. If you're interested in using them in your own playing, there's lots of useful information about them in the essential books of Phil Ochs and Clare McKenna and - of course - on the internet.

The Cut

The **Cut** is the ornament most easy to play. In the terms of classical music it's a grace note played rapidly before the main note. The **cut** or grace note has no distinct time value and is always **higher** than the main note.

The Tap

The **Tap** is another basic ornament. It's played just like the cut, e.g. as a short grace note of no distinct duration rapidly preceding the main note. In contrast to the cut the tap is always **deeper** than the main note.

The Double Cut or Casadh

The **Casadh** is quite similar to the cut but starts on the main note. It consists of two grace notes rapidly played before the main note.

C
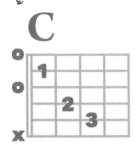

C⁷
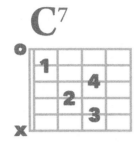

Cm
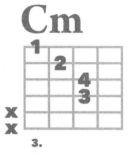

Cm (alternate Fingering)

C♯m
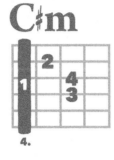

D
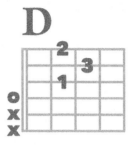

D⁷

Dm
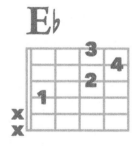

E♭
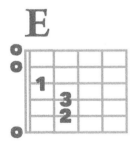

E

E⁷
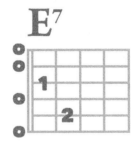

Em
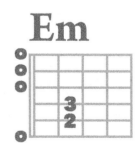

F
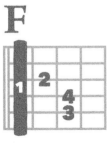

F (alternate Fingering)
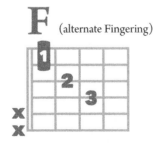

F⁷
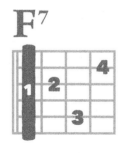

Fm
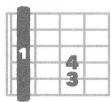

F#m
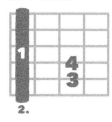

G
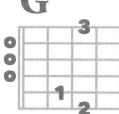

G (Griffvariante)

G⁷
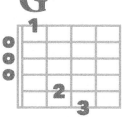

Gm
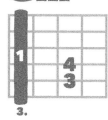

A
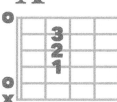

A⁷
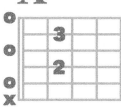

A⁷ (alternate Fingering)
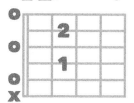

Am
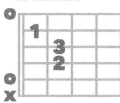

B♭
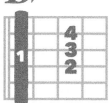

B
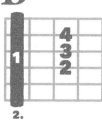

B (alternate Fingering)
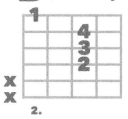

B⁷
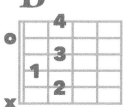

Bm
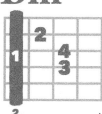

Strumming patterns for guitar

The following is a selection of basic strumming pattern which you can use for song accompaniment. These are just for starters – you'll soon use other, more elaborate pattern or invent your own. Feel free to use a pick or your finger(s) for strumming – basically whatever feels best.

Here's how they're read:

- The horizontal lines represent the strings of your guitar.
  Downstroke (strumming in the direction of the floor): arrow upward
  Upstroke: arrow downward.
- The length of the arrows indicates which strings to strum.
- Each of these pattern shows a whole measure.

For song accompaniment you can choose (and also combine) whatever pattern feels best to you, but keep in mind to match the pattern's time to the time of the song, e.g. for a song in 4/4 time only use strumming patterns in 4/4 time.
Songs in 2/2 time can be played using strumming patterns in 4/4 time.

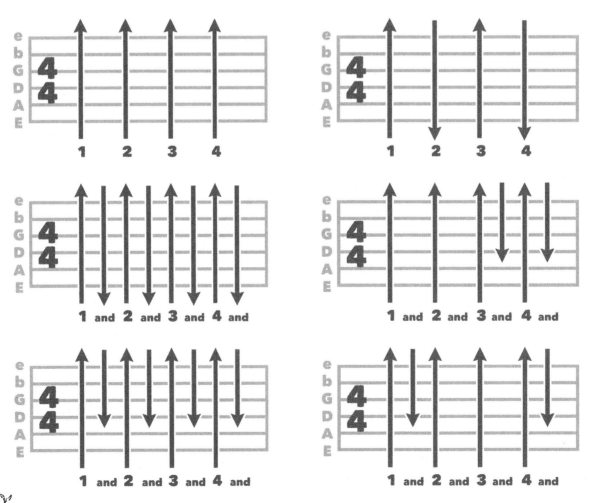

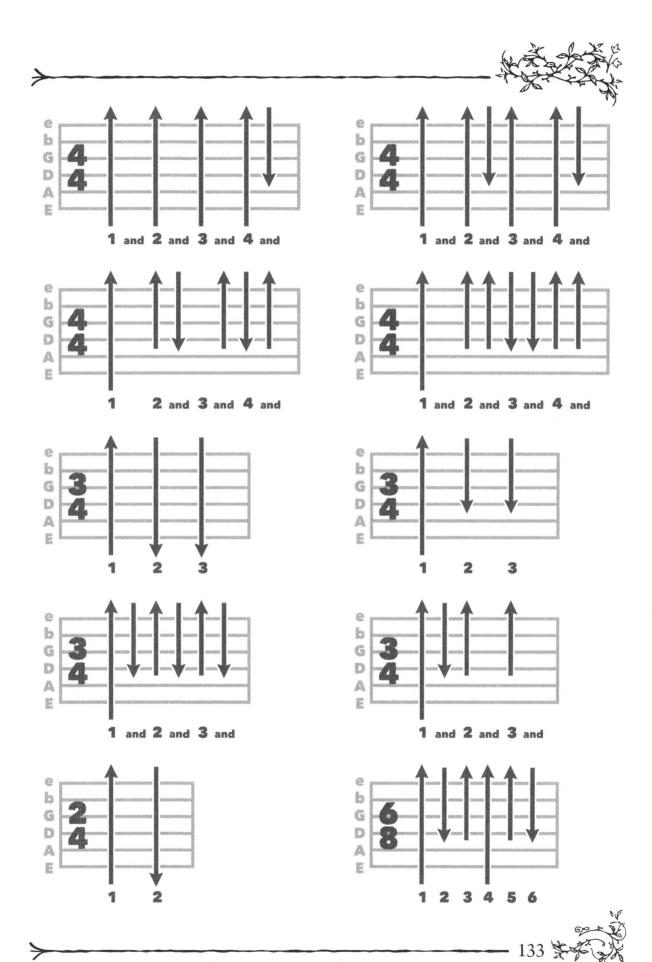

Picking patterns for guitar

A lot of songs sound particularly good when played using a picking pattern. Here's the basic idea: instead of picking all the notes of a chord simultaneously with your finger(s) or a pick, you play them successively, one after the other. Picking patterns are commonly used for longer musical sections (or even whole songs) and adapted to the chord changes if necessary. Here's an example, using the A minor chord:

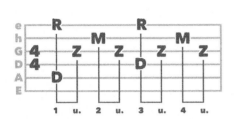
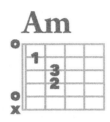

As in tablature, horizontal lines represent the strings of your guitar. The time signature is notated at the beginning of the pattern as a fraction (here: 4/4; this is a pattern for songs in 4/4 time). The letters T, I, M and R indicate the fingers of the picking hand. Below the pattern I've notated how to count it. Here's a step-by-step explanation of the above example:
- on the first beat ("1") the ring finger picks the e string.
- on the second half of the first beat ("1and") the index finger picks the G string.
- on the second beat ("2") the middle finger picks the b string.
- on the second half of the second beat ("2and") the index finger picks the G string once again.
- On the third beat, thumb and ring finger simultaneously pick the D and the e string.
and so on …

There are a few basic things to keep in mind when using picking patterns:
Obviously, the pattern's time signature has to match that of the song. In some cases, the pattern has to be adapted to a certain chord or a chord change, but most of the time you can use the following simple rule:
• pick the bass strings (6th, 5th and 4th) string with your thumb,
• pick the G (3rd) string with your index finger,
• the B (2nd) string with your middle finger and
• the e (1st) string with your ring finger.

One of the best ways to practise picking patterns is to play them on open strings until the movement of your fingers becomes second nature – practicing this way ensures you'll be able to concentrate on more important things when it's time to play the song.
When the picking pattern has been "automized" to a certain degree it's time to add chords and chord changes. Take your time because nothing sounds worse than a "stuttering" picking pattern interfering with a smooth chord change.
On the following pages you'll find some basic picking patterns to choose from. Of course, this is just a small selection from the multitude of possible patterns, meant to whet your appetite – you'll soon find varying patterns and inventing new ones of your own can be lots of fun!

For a start, you may want to try:

• Combining different picking patterns
  (e. g. one for the verse and one for the chorus).
• Combining picking patterns with strumming patterns.
• Mixing picking patterns with melody lines and damping techniques.
• Playing some of your favorites "backwards".

Sometimes you'll encounter indications in Spanish:
P (pulgar) = Thumb
I (indice) = Index finger
M (medio) = Middle finger
A (anular) = Ring finger

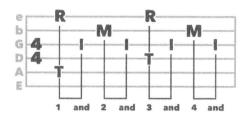
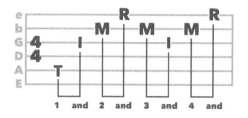

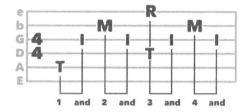
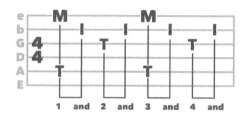

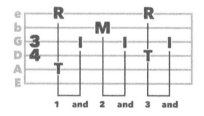
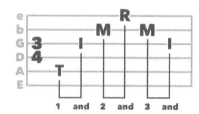

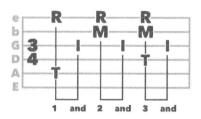
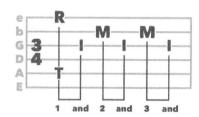

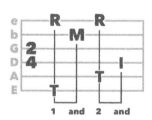
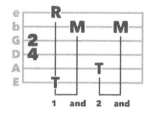

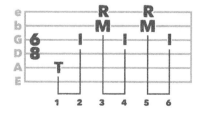
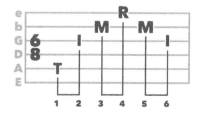

Made in the USA
Monee, IL
20 July 2023

39645067R00077